THE DOCTORS WHO CONQUERED
YELLOW FEVER

THE DOCTORS WHO
CONQUERED
YELLOW FEVER

★

by **RALPH NADING HILL**

Illustrated by **R. M. POWERS**

Landmark BOOKS

RANDOM HOUSE · NEW YORK

For the Durick family

ACKNOWLEDGMENT

Dr. George K. Strode, formerly director of the International Health Division of the Rockefeller Foundation, and Dr. Philip S. Hench, senior consultant of the department of arthritis at the Mayo Clinic—two of the foremost authorities on yellow fever—have kindly given many hours of the most vital assistance in the preparation of this book. They have my lasting gratitude.

R.N.H.

CONTENTS

THE DOCTORS WHO CONQUERED
YELLOW FEVER

1

A TEEN-AGED DOCTOR

If the hills of Virginia lay even greener in the morning sun on September 13, 1851, Pharaba Reed and her husband, Parson Reed, were too busy to notice them. The baby born to them that day was their fifth. He seemed no different from the others. In the stories of Walter Reed's childhood there is no hint of the man whose name would be inscribed one day in the Hall of Fame. Like any other small boy he easily wandered in and out of trouble.

On one occasion he went with friends on a tour of the tobacco houses of Farmville in Gloucester County. It was not long before the older boys in the group, wearing their usual badge of importance, tasted the tobacco. Chewing and spitting like old farmhands, they dared Walter to follow suit. He bravely stuffed a bitter sample into his mouth, chewed, spat, and bit off some more—feeling quite a man of the world. But then, gradually, his newfound confidence ebbed away. The ground began to reel upward and his face turned white as chalk. He sank down in the purest misery and soon would not talk, walk or crawl.

Fearful because of what had happened and because they were in a forbidden place, the older boys carried Walter to a spot some distance away from the tobacco shed. Here they begged him to stand up and walk, but he could not. He appeared to be very ill indeed.

"Promise, Walter," implored one of the older boys, "that you will not tell even if it kills you."

Weakly the younger boy moved his lips. "Even if I die," he promised, "I will not tell." Reassured, his companions picked him up again and struggled toward his home.

The effects of this escapade soon wore off and it was Walter's last childhood encounter with tobacco. He would scarcely have been a normal youth, however, if he had not found himself in further trouble of a different kind. One such occasion was in 1865, during the Civil War, when Sheridan and his Raiders galloped through the Virginia countryside sweeping southern livestock before them. Walter and an older brother named Christopher, together with a neighborhood friend, were sent off to hide their parents' horses. They found a spot on the river bend beside a deep, crescent-shaped swimming hole. Resolving to camp

there until the danger passed, they tied their horses inside a thick screen of trees and bushes. The river beckoned and they wasted little time ashore that day.

One morning when they were in for a dip the clattering of hooves sounded along the bank. Before the boys had time to think, Sheridan's Raiders, led to their hiding place by an untrustworthy servant, burst into the thicket and seized their horses.

Hustling the panic-stricken boys out of the water and into their clothes, the Raiders led them away. There was the greatest anguish among their families that night. Fortunately the prisoners were considered too young to keep. They joyfully reached their homes on foot, but the horses were gone forever.

Except for that rather dramatic episode, Walter Reed had a typical southern boyhood, but soon began to show the traits that proved so valuable in the great drama of his life. From the time he was old enough to suspect how interesting and worthwhile the life of a doctor could be, he never doubted that that was what he wanted to become. Anxious to learn, he was so clever and persistent in his studies that he entered the University of Virginia at the age of sixteen. But financial difficulties arose. Walter's father, who drew only the modest salary of a Methodist minister, was already sending two older sons to college and could not afford to send a third for more than one year.

To abandon his studies meant giving up a career as a doctor, and Walter resolved not to do that. Gathering his courage, he appeared before the faculty.

"If I study medicine for the next nine months and pass your examinations," he asked them, "will you give me a degree?"

The astonished professors smiled at one another. A sixteen-year-old with only one year of Latin, Greek and English literature proposing to study medicine! He could not possibly pass! Therefore the professors felt safe in granting his request.

"Doctor Maupin," Walter said, addressing the chairman, "you have heard what these gentlemen say. Will you see that I have my degree of M.D. if I meet the requirements?"

"If you pass the examinations," agreed the doctor, "you will receive a degree."

"Gentlemen," said Walter, "I hold you to your promise."

The dignity with which the boy conducted

himself could not help but impress the professors. Yet after he had gone they again broke into broad smiles. The requirements for a medical degree in those days were not so rigid as they are now, but at the University of Virginia, which had one of the first schools of medicine in the country, the subjects were difficult and the professors exacting. No boy, however bright, could vault through the course in nine months!

So thought the professors. They did not know Walter Reed. His older brother, Christopher, with whom he roomed during the nine months he had allotted for the study of medicine, reported that Walter sometimes allowed himself only three hours' sleep out of twenty-four. But when the time for his examinations came he was ready. And after correcting his papers, his professors were amazed to find that he ranked third highest in his class.

So the proud day dawned when Walter Reed, at the tender age of 17, became a doctor.

"You are the youngest student who ever graduated from the Charlottesville Medical School," said Dr. Maupin, presenting Walter with his diploma. "You have met every requirement, and the faculty is bound in honor to award this degree to you."

2

THE OBSTACLE RACE
AND THE BEARDLESS RUNNER

We all want the world to think well of us, and Walter was no exception. He yearned to work among the sick, and dreamed of lighting up some shadowy corner of the underworld of disease.

A century ago the science of medicine was still in its infancy. People died by the thousands of simple appendicitis. Dreadful fevers swept whole families away, while doctors stood by helplessly. If a person was desperately ill he was not given blood—it was drawn out of him. One needed the strength of Atlas to survive an operation, which was performed with clumsy instruments by a surgeon wearing the same bloodstained coat he might have worn for months. Few doctors dreamed that unsanitary instruments conveyed deadly germs, for Pasteur and Lister had not yet shown the importance of antisepsis. Although the nature of many infectious diseases was known, the ways by which they were transmitted were not understood. Like the ranges of the West awaiting hopeful prospectors, the frontiers of medicine beckoned to explorers who were willing to learn, to work and to sacrifice.

New York was the center for those seeking medical experience. And no more eager student than Walter Reed ever left home to glean knowledge and experience in the strange confusion of

New York City. With the wonderful feeling that he was almost a full-fledged doctor, he continued his studies in Bellevue Hospital Medical College. Then, as a part-time resident on the staffs of several hospitals in the city, he began to practice what he had learned.

But now came a time of great unhappiness. He was appointed district physician in one of the poorest areas of the city. Day and night he labored among the sick and dirty tenement buildings filled with disease and vice. One night, according to Christopher Reed, who by this time was a lawyer in New York, Walter returned to their apartment very late. Not yet asleep, Christopher watched his younger brother go to the window and look sadly down upon the streets. For a long time he stood silent and then, as if to wash away the wickedness of the city, he began to quote from the Bible. Then he kneeled beside his bed and slowly and with great emotion recited the Lord's Prayer.

The wretched atmosphere in which he worked was not, however, the only reason for Walter's unhappiness. His youthfulness was a distinct handicap. Although he was a competent surgeon, wiser than many who were twice his age, he looked too young to be a doctor. Patients entering his office were so startled when they saw his boyish face and figure that they often turned away to seek the advice of older men. "A doctor's success," he wrote a friend, "depends more upon his beard than his brains." Since Walter could not grow a beard ample enough to disguise his face, he had to put up with his youthful appearance as best he could, and to suffer many depressing experiences.

At the age of 22, when he was serving as one of the five inspectors on the Brooklyn Board of Health, he came home one night feeling very depressed. When Christopher asked what the trouble was, Walter said: "Today an elegant carriage with a coachman and footman stopped in front of my office. One of Brooklyn's wealthy doctors, dressed in the finest clothes, got out, knocked on my door and introduced himself. He said he wanted to report the death of a child. When I asked him what the child died of, he could not tell me. He could not even tell what the symptoms were, to say nothing of using medical terms correctly.

"I then asked him if he did not think it was such-and-such a disease, using the Latin term. 'Yes, that was it,' he told me, and repeated the Latin term backward.

"This man," continued Walter, "has the leading practice in this part of Brooklyn, yet he is a first-class quack. I am disgusted and feel like giving up my profession."

He did not really mean that, of course. The practice of medicine was his whole life. But since building up a practice in the city seemed to be almost an impossibility for a man so young, he had about decided to close his office. For some time he had thought of trying to gain an appointment in the Army Medical Corps, for this would assure him a regular income. A regular income was necessary if a young man was to support a wife. And Walter had met Emilie Lawrence, a young lady whom he wanted most ardently to support. He had met her on a visit to his father's and had known her only a month, but during that brief time he had thought about her constantly.

At last he made his decision. It was a happy one for his career and fateful for the history of medicine. To enter the Army Medical Corps— for that was what he had decided to do—he had to pass examinations not only in medicine, but also in Latin, Greek, mathematics, literature and history. Since Walter had attended college only one year, he felt doomed to fail in all these subjects. Every night for weeks he pored over his books, stuffing his head so full of information that it seemed to him it might explode. But how else was he to win one of thirty openings for which many more young doctors were competing? There may have been a time when he could study twenty hours a day, but no longer. He became sick, went to bed for three weeks and missed his examinations. Taking up his studies too soon after his illness, he became sick again. Fortunately the Army provided a third opportunity and in February, 1875, he finally appeared before the examining board.

The horrors of answering questions five hours a day for six straight days can well be imagined by any student who has had to stand up and recite long passages by heart. Hopeful, grimfaced young doctors from all over the country—some in ten-gallon hats, some in Prince Albert coats and broad-brimmed felt hats, and some in threadbare country suits—nervously began their recitations before the uniformed medical officers.

By the second day some of the candidates were gone. Four days later most of them had packed their carpet bags or their black leather valises and started glumly back to their homes. But of the hundreds of applicants there remained a few outstanding ones. Walter Reed was one of them. He passed his examinations brilliantly and in June, 1875, at the age of 24, was awarded a commission as assistant surgeon in the United States Medical Corps with the rank of first lieutenant. The bleak years of struggle for an education lay behind him and he had fond hopes for the future—for Emilie had agreed to become his wife.

Just before he was to be married, however, his rainbow disappeared in storm clouds. The Army ordered him to Indian country in Arizona. He himself did not mind going there, but he could not imagine Emilie living on the frontier. Well, he was not going to put off his marriage! He asked for and received an appointment with the Surgeon-General. This is a very unusual thing to have happen in the Army Medical Corps. It is as if a schoolboy who is a safety patrolman called on the city chief of police.

"Sit down!" the Surgeon-General of the United States ordered lowly Lieutenant Walter Reed. Walter sat down.

"What do you want?" demanded the General.

"I would like to know, General," said Walter in a voice that betrayed his nervousness, "if I can get a leave in Arizona. I am engaged and would like to return from there to be married."

The General's expression was grim. "Young man, if you don't want to go to Arizona, resign from the service!" Now flared the spirit Walter had shown 'way back when he sought a degree before the University of Virginia faculty.

"General," he replied, "I did not work for my commission as hard as I did just to throw it away hastily. Nor can you deprive me of it till I act so unworthily as to cause dismissal."

The General's eyebrows went up. Then the lines in his face softened, evidently in amusement at the spirit Walter showed. "Have a cigar, Dr.

Reed," he said, "and let us talk it over." The General did most of the talking and his final advice to Walter was: "Don't marry now. Go to Arizona. You will have a chance to come back before long."

From what he had heard of the Army, Walter did not share the General's optimism about the chance of a fairly early leave. He promptly married Emilie—in April, 1876—and left for the far west two weeks later. In October Emilie started off across the continent to join him.

3

CANYON COUNTRY ADVENTURES

A blizzard and a train wreck did not prevent
Emilie, a high-spirited girl of 20, from reaching
Walter in San Diego where he had gone to meet
her. In mid-November of 1876 the couple started
off in a mule-drawn army wagon on a 22-day
journey to Walter's new post at Fort Lowell,

Arizona. The road was so bad that by five o'clock in the afternoon of the first day they had gone only ten miles, and Walter had found it necessary to lead the mules every step of the way.

By midnight they had not yet reached the road station where they planned to sleep. Ahead lay a canyon which fell steeply away from the narrow road of sand strewn with boulders. Carrying a lantern whose feeble light penetrated only a few feet through the blackness, Walter plunged forward knee-deep in sand, shouting back directions to the driver of the team: "Now to the right! Now left!" Every so often Emilie worriedly called out: "Where are you! Please come back and let the soldier carry the lantern!" But Walter was afraid that his wagon with its precious cargo might go over the cliff. He would trust no one to lead the team and struggled on alone.

Safely threading their way through the winding canyon they at last saw light streaming through the cracks of a cabin, which turned out

to be the road station they sought. Only ten feet square, the tiny building was constructed of rough boards awkwardly joined together. The ceiling was of dirt plastered over roof boards, the floor was of dirt, and the furniture consisted of a stool, a broken chair, a pine table, a cooking stove and a bed made of canvas stretched over a frame. The lonely fellow who kept the station greeted the Reeds warmly, prepared some tea, gave Walter and Emilie his "bed," and would not charge them a cent.

The following night they stopped at a similar hut and were greeted by a caretaker. He told the

newlyweds he was taking the place of the original keeper whom he had found lying outside the door with a bullet through his heart.

"The coyotes have about finished him," announced the caretaker, pointing to the bones near by, "and I hope the young lady will not be afeared of his arm bone. I use it to prop open the window." In this, there was an element of grim humor. Both Walter and his young wife had to smile, when she could have cried just as easily.

At last they reached Fort Lowell, a primitive outpost which was to be their home for a year. Since Walter was the only doctor for miles around, he cared not only for the troops as an army surgeon, but also for the far-spread settlers who called him out on the desert or the mesa day and night in all kinds of weather.

Yet in many ways Fort Lowell was better than the next post, Camp Apache, which was 700 miles from the railroad with mail service only once a week by stage.

In the summer of 1877 the Reeds started for this remote station in an "ambulance," a wagon painted white to repel the fierce heat of the desert. Although another wagon containing nearly 2,000 pounds of their belongings had left ahead of them the day before, the ambulance creaked with cargo as the mules strained to set it in motion for its long journey. On the back seat sat Walter, Emilie and their dog, Undina. Under the back seat was a box of medicines for emergencies, a lunch basket, a jar of preserved ginger, a pair of boots, a blacking brush, and a bag containing a saucepan, frying pan, tin pan and coffee pot. On the front seat were two folding chairs, Walter's valise, a bundle of shawls, an overcoat, two double blankets, a feather pillow, a clothes brush and four books. Under the front seat was a mess chest containing tableware, a box of provisions and a large clothes basket filled with odds and ends. Hanging from the roof were two hats, a sword, an umbrella, shoes, a carbine, a pistol, a cartridge belt and two canteens filled with water. Forward, underneath the driver's seat, was a doctor's case of instruments weighing fifty pounds, a sack of grain and the driver's rations for ten days. Among still other articles were a trunk and a gigantic roll of bedding—mattress, blankets, and sheets—covered over with canvas. And the driver shared his seat with an Army corporal who weighed 200 pounds!

In a letter describing this journey to his wife's sister, Walter Reed told of the worst road in the world. "Imagine," he wrote, "a steep hill covered with stones the size of flour barrels, packed just as closely as possible, some on end, some on their sides, and some on their edges." The only way the travelers could descend the hill without upsetting the wagon was to attach strong ropes on each side. When the wheels on one side passed over a boulder, raising the wagon to a dangerous angle, the men pulled down on that side with the ropes as hard as they could.

At the foot of the hill they found the heavy wagon which had started a day earlier. It was so embedded in boulders that its large team of twelve mules, aided by the four that were pulling the ambulance, were able to drag it only thirty feet in seven hours. It was necessary to unpack the wagon and carry part of the load piecemeal on the backs of the mules.

An even steeper hill lay ahead—the steepest hill in the world on the worst road in the world, according to Walter. In order to keep the wagon from pitching downward end over end, the men locked the wheels and dragged a large tree behind it. Even then it was touch and go with all hands helping to hold it back with ropes. At one point, where there was a sheer drop of five feet, the soles of Walter's shoes were torn off as he skidded behind the wagon.

On a long journey such as this, occupying many days, Indian attacks constantly threatened, but the Reeds seemed to lead charmed lives. One night they camped on a plain where only three days later two tribes of Indians engaged in a frightful battle. On another occasion Walter decided at the last moment not to ride in a stage-coach whose driver was killed in an ambush a few hours later.

During the journey to Camp Apache an Indian who turned out to be the famous "Dead-Shot" (so named because he never missed his mark) appeared and asked for something to eat. He was given a loaf of hard bread which he ate in its entirety, and went happily on his way.

The life of a doctor, of course, was far safer than that of the average white settler, for the Indians had learned that many Army surgeons would treat them as willingly as they would the troops for whose health they were responsible. Many a time Walter packed his saddlebags and rode off into the night, not to mend the broken bone of a white man or prescribe for his fevered child, but to treat a sick Indian. The redman would repay him by stealing softly into his house, removing a picture from the wall, and hanging up a haunch of venison in its stead.

On one journey a detachment of soldiers from Fort Apache found a young Indian girl who had been terribly burned and had been abandoned by her tribe. The soldiers wrapped her in blankets, which they pinned together with horseshoe nails, and carried her back to camp on an improvised litter. With the tenderest care Walter succeeded in nursing her back to health. Suzie—as she was called—remained for a number of years as a companion for the Reeds' young son, Walter Lawrence, but when she had almost grown up she returned to her Apache people to teach them English.

If life on the western frontier was one of hardship, however, there were certain rewards as well.

31

During his three years in Arizona Walter learned much about human nature. Then as now, a doctor's wisdom was gained not so much in the classroom or laboratory as among his patients, and Walter treated thousands of the sick, encountering every ailment to be found in the Southwest.

Six weeks before his promotion in June, 1880 to captain, he received orders to proceed East. The telegram from Army headquarters read: "You will proceed north to the Union Pacific Railroad, striking the railroad between Cheyenne and Salt Lake City." The Reeds packed their belongings and set out once again on another very tedious journey over trackless land.

One day they discovered that their Indian girl, Suzie, was missing. She had last been seen peacefully sleeping in a clothes basket on the back of the army wagon. An alarm was sounded and the small caravan ground to a halt while the men turned about to search the trail behind them. They found

Suzie on the ground one-half mile back, still in her clothes basket, and still asleep!

When they finally reached the railroad one of the enlisted men removed his red flannel undershirt and flagged the train. As it wheezed to a stop Walter shouted to the conductor that he was heading East on Army orders. The next train West would bring the doctor replacing him at Fort Apache. He would take over the wagon train that had brought the Reeds to the railroad.

When the family at last stepped off the train in New York after a rattling and sooty trip across the country, Emilie was carrying young Walter, while Captain Reed was leading the little Indian girl by the hand.

"Good Heavens!" a bystander was heard to remark. "Look at that combination!"

After serving five months at Fort Ontario, New York, Walter was ordered to Fort McHenry near Baltimore. This pleased him, for Johns Hopkins

University was near by and presented to him the brightest prospect of his Army career. The first biological laboratory in the country had been established there. Excitement filled the atmosphere. Louis Pasteur had opened astonishing vistas in the world beneath the microscope. Captain Reed yearned to know the secrets that were unfolding there. Yet he had chosen the life of an Army doctor. After only a tantalizing few months spent at the threshold of Johns Hopkins, he had no choice but to pack up and move to his next station, Washington, D. C.

He was soon ordered West again, this time to Fort Omaha, Nebraska. For five more years he moved about from one dreary western post to another, a country doctor in uniform ministering to the needs of the poor farmers who lived on the wind-swept plains. Often, as he harnessed his horse on a winter's night and rode off into the bitter cold to the cabin of a sick ranger, he despaired that he would ever again see the inside of a laboratory. He had given his work the fullest devotion. He had joined the Army and had cheerfully gone where he had been sent. But he was beginning to wonder if he was to spend his entire Army career at the ragged edges of the American frontier.

Finally, in 1887, he was ordered east to Alabama. Here with his growing family (a daughter had been born to Emilie in 1883) he spent three pleasant years in his southern homeland. In 1890 he found himself back in Baltimore as Examiner of Recruits. As he had done ten years before, he seized this opportunity by spending every spare moment at Johns Hopkins.

During his long absence in the West the medical world had marched steadily forward, and Walter felt rather like a recruit in the rear ranks. The discoveries of Pasteur and Robert Koch, proving that tiny bacteria caused such diseases as tuberculosis and diphtheria, had become widely accepted. Having seen and identified these microscopic foes of mankind, scientists were beginning to fight them.

Luck may have forsaken Walter Reed out West, but now it showered him with opportunities. At Johns Hopkins he studied under one of the most forward-looking doctors in the world—William Welch. Welch had had the good fortune to study abroad. Now, as professor of bacteriology and pathology at Johns Hopkins, he was sharing the world's knowledge with men whose strongest appetites were their thirst for learning and their hunger for pure research. In the laboratory with Welch were other prominent doctors—William Halstead, William Osler and Howard Kelly—men whose influence was helping to lift medicine out of the Dark Ages.

As Walter labored over his test tubes and slides on the laboratory table allotted to him, the heat of the desert and the cracking cold of the north-western prairie seemed to belong to some other age and the life of some other man. He knew that this was his real work, for he was so very happy doing it. Although his young son Walter was away at school, his wife and small daughter lived near by. For the doctor, a stimulating day of work at the laboratory ended in a comfortable evening with his family. Although inclined to be dignified and reserved among casual acquaintances or associates he was warm and full of fun, even of horseplay, when with his family or close friends. Once, to the delight of his daughter, he seized the paws of the family cat and waltzed him around the Christmas tree.

But an Army surgeon could not spend much time at the hearthside. From time to time during his very brief tour of duty at Baltimore Walter was reminded that no station is permanent in the Army, for he would again be ordered away on temporary duty.

Yet in his relatively short time at the laboratory he distinguished himself and changed the course of his life. While examining victims of typhoid fever, he had discovered that they all had lumps in the lymph-glands of the liver. He sought to learn and did learn what they were: groups of dead liver cells. He succeeded experimentally in producing the lumps in the laboratory's animals. This by itself was no great discovery, but it demonstrated to Dr. Welch that here was a clever student, inquisitive, resourceful and persistent.

So while Walter was out West again during what may have seemed two more years of exile, the work he did at Johns Hopkins was speaking for him: it became known in Army medical circles. In 1893, after 18 years and fifteen changes of station, his garrison life ended. He was ordered to Washington, promoted to major and to the rank of full surgeon and made director of the Army Medical Library. To his delight he was also named professor of bacteriology at the new United States Army Medical School.

Thus did he abandon forever the life of the practicing physician to share the twin delights of research work and teaching. "You can accomplish so much more good for so many more people by training other men in modern medicine," he remarked one day to Emilie. "That's what counts with me. I might be able to save ten children strangling with diphtheria, but if I teach ten men to use antitoxin, they can save a hundred."

4

THE BLACK TRACK OF YELLOW JACK

In the old days the patent-medicine salesman was a familiar sight on the village green. In a side-show voice he shouted that his tonic was equally good for stomach ache or fever. It would dry up a cold and banish warts. The salesman soon had more eager buyers for his worthless remedy than a popcorn vendor at a baseball game.

The medical scholars—the Walter Reeds—are to be thanked for ridding us of the patent-medicine salesmen and for making the practice of medicine much more scientific. This was a great achievement because only a generation ago there was much ignorance even among the doctors themselves. In 1898 when Major Reed was appointed chairman of a committee to study typhoid fever, five different doctors gave five different opinions as to the cause of that disease. Even though one doctor might *prove* his theory and make his proof as clear as the midday sun, the others would cling stubbornly to their own opinions for a long time thereafter.

In some ways the study of medicine is as exact a science as that of mathematics. But at the time Walter Reed undertook to find the causes of typhoid fever among the troops in the Spanish-American War, there were so many unknown factors in the study of infectious diseases that medicine could not yet be called a science.

After many months of careful, often tedious work in the Army camps Major Reed and two colleagues, Doctors Shakespeare and Vaughan, reported that typhoid was spread by the common fly, by contact with persons who had the disease, by infected articles such as drinking and eating utensils, and by contaminated drinking water.

The survey of the camps had not long been completed before Reed was asked to make a study of yellow fever, an equally dreadful disease, found mainly in the tropics or sub-tropics. A person attacked by it suffered chills and fever at first; he might even be sick at his stomach and suffer headache and backache pains. Jaundice might turn his skin yellow. If he vomited blood he usually died within a few days.

For at least two centuries prior to the time Walter Reed waged war on yellow fever, this disease had ravaged Africa, Europe and the Americas. In the beginning doctors had been absolutely helpless against it and all that could be done was to

bury the dead. The first terrible epidemic thought
to have been caused by yellow fever took place
among the Mayan Indians in Yucatan in 1648.
Early in June of that year, according to a writer
then living, there rolled over the country a dense
fog which to the old Indians was a sure sign of
death. Then in the city of Campeche yellow fever
struck. It spread so fast that within a short time
it had paralyzed the entire city.

All roads were guarded to keep people from
leaving Campeche. Despite this quarantine the
disease spread to Meriden in August. "With such
quickness and violence it came on great and little,
rich and poor, that in less than eight days almost
the whole city was sick at one time and many of
the citizens of the highest name and authority in
it died."

The following year the disease spread to the
island of Cuba and killed one-third of the inhabitants. In 1665 it claimed the lives of all but 89
of an English squadron of 1,500 men on the

island of St. Lucia. Between 1702 and 1878 "Yellow Jack" visited southern and Atlantic Coast cities in the United States no less than 112 times. So frightful was its spread through Philadelphia in 1793 that one out of every ten persons died. The daily affairs of the city were strangled. For fear of catching the disease friends avoided one another in the streets and would not shake hands. People withdrew into their houses and closed the

blinds, but the disease sought them out there and often destroyed an entire family within a few days. In New Orleans more than 8,000 citizens died of yellow fever in 1853. On a rampage through the Mississippi Valley twenty-five years later, it killed *thirteen thousand* people.

And nothing could be done about it. The enemy was unseen; its hiding places and habits were unknown. Doctors had many theories. Since yellow fever always seemed to strike along the water's edge, some thought that it was caused by mud from the docks, or dead dogs, cats and horses, or decay of some kind. Some doctors claimed that heat, moisture and filth brought on an epidemic. Some said it was due to the "Yellow Fever Breeze" and others to the Gulf Stream. Some were sure that a certain kind of fungus was the culprit. Oranges and bananas were also blamed. There was a whole group who held that the disease resulted from a poison that exploded in the air. Others said flatly that one person could not catch it from another. For those whom Yellow Jack did strike, whiskey and mustard seed, brandy and cigars were thought to be good remedies. There was, in short, no knowledge and no remedy—only ignorance and fear. With torches and tarpots burning and large cannon firing to "expel the poisoned air," the streets of an infected city bore a ghostly and mournful appearance.

Because the year 1899 was not "clear and beautiful" the Cubans were saying that 1900 was going to be a "Yellow Fever Year" on their island. Perhaps Walter Reed thought so too, for after many long months of inquiry he was ordered to seek out the yellow plague in the heart of its stronghold—the island of Cuba.

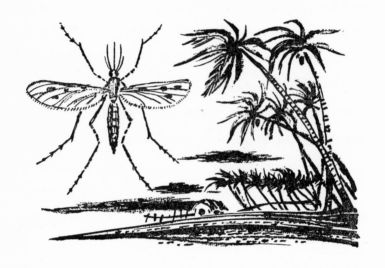

5

OPENING FIRE AT LOS QUEMADOS

Shortly before noon on New Year's day, 1899, the regulars and volunteers of the Eighth and Tenth Regiments, United States Army, marched to the park facing the Havana palace of the Governor-General of Cuba. Here they snapped to attention behind their officers, who were sitting erect in the saddles on their fine horses. Drawn up on the opposite side of the park were forces of Her Majesty, Christine, Queen-Regent of Spain.

At the stroke of noon the red-and-yellow Spanish flag on the Governor-General's palace was lowered and the Stars and Stripes went up. As General Blanco formally surrendered his power on the balcony of the palace, bands played the national anthems of the United States and Spain. In the harbor near by thunderous volleys echoed from American warships.

Officially the Spanish-American War was over. But for the soldiers of the medical corps in charge of the health of American occupation forces, the "fighting" had just begun. Lurking on rooftops, in narrow alleyways and in a thousand dark corners of the city was Yellow Jack, an enemy far mightier than Spain.

In July of 1898 it had struck the men of the Second Coast Artillery. Of those who became ill, one-third died. With the number of cases in and about Havana mounting alarmingly, General Leonard Wood moved the Eighth Infantry to Columbia Barracks at Los Quemados, a post situated on a sunny, wind-swept plateau which sloped gradually toward the Gulf of Mexico. For a while things went well in this open area but in the spring of 1900 the Cubans' fateful prediction that this was to be a Yellow Fever Year began to come true. At number 20, General Lee Street in Quemados, a case of yellow fever appeared only a few hundred yards from the Columbia Barracks hospital. Then, curiously enough, instead of spreading to the nearby houses it struck several houses away on the next street, Calzada Real.

A feeling of anxiety seized the officers of the medical corps, for Los Quemados was one of the cleanest villages in Cuba and the army post nearby was considered to be in a healthful location. Every possible measure had been taken to ward off disease. The instructions of Major William C. Gorgas, chief surgeon of the department of Havana, had been carried out to the letter. The drinking water was fresh and the sewage system good. All fever patients had been separated from the other troops and housed in special buildings. These measures had controlled malaria and typhoid. Unfortunately, they had no effect on Yellow Jack. Like shipwrecked men the medical officers at Columbia Barracks watched the yellow tidal wave roll toward them as summer drew near.

At this point, on June 25, 1900, Major Walter Reed arrived from Washington. Within a day he and the other members of the Yellow Fever Board, just appointed by Army Surgeon-General Sternberg, were at work. Reed was the presiding officer of this medical task force. Serving with him were a Cuban named Aristides Agramonte, James Carroll, long a co-worker with Reed, and Jesse Lazear, a graduate of Johns Hopkins who was now in charge of the laboratory at Camp Columbia.

For some time before Major Reed's arrival Jesse Lazear had been hard at work investigating the blood of persons ill with yellow fever at Quemados. Indeed, all of the Board members were familiar with the character of the disease, for all except Lazear had helped Surgeon-General Sternberg, long an expert, to disprove false theories as to its origin. The difficult task of Walter Reed and his Yellow Fever Board was to discover, if possible, the cause of the disease. For unless that were done there was little hope of rooting it out of the pesthole of Cuba.

Although it was known in 1900 that mosquitoes spread malaria from one person to another, Board Member Jesse Lazear was but one of three scientists who had suspected that they also might carry yellow fever. And yet, scattered through medical history there were isolated reports of other students who had at least mentioned such a possibility.

For example, in the early days of our republic Noah Webster, who was not a doctor at all but father of the *American Spelling Book* and of the famous dictionary bearing his name, wrote: "I think it proper here to remark that in the year 1795, when the weather was excessively hot and the air humid, about the time yellow fever made its appearance in [New York], it was observed that flies disappeared and mosquitoes invaded us in numberless swarms. Flies delight in hot, dry air —mosquitoes in hot, moist air, and wherever the latter abound, it may be considered that the air is not [healthful]."

In 1848 Dr. Josiah C. Nott of Mobile, Alabama, wrote that he was convinced some insect must carry the yellow fever germ.

When Walter Reed arrived in Cuba there lived in Havana an able and accomplished doctor named Carlos J. Finlay. For years he had tried to convince people, through his writing on the subject, that yellow fever was spread by the female *Aedes aegypti*, a "domestic" mosquito that lived in and around human dwellings.

Very soon after he arrived in Cuba Major Reed and some of his staff went to see Dr. Finlay, a kindly old gentleman with white side-whiskers. For almost twenty years he had been raising mosquitoes in glass jars and dissecting them under a microscope. There was little doubt in Finlay's mind that mosquitoes carried Yellow Jack by biting a person who was ill with the disease and carrying it to others by biting them in turn. Having long studied the life cycle of the domestic mosquito, he was aware that conditions had to be just right for this insect to spread the disease. The temperature of the air could not be too cold or too hot. If it was too cold, the mosquitoes died; if it was too hot, they became inactive. Moreover, it appeared that in order to carry yellow fever they had to bite a person ill with the disease a certain number of days *after he had come down with it*. Otherwise the germ would not be passed along to the mosquito. Finlay also suspected that the mosquito might be unable to convey Yellow Jack to others until a certain number of days had passed *after it had bitten the infected person*. He was not sure of this timing but of one thing he was certain: if domestic mosquitoes were annihilated, or if people were protected from being bitten by them there would be no more yellow fever.

To prove his theories the Cuban doctor conducted no less than 103 experiments on human beings, using home-grown mosquitoes that he had allowed to bite victims of yellow fever. For some reason only sixteen of all those bitten contracted what Finlay at least thought was experimental yellow fever. For nineteen years the whole scientific world had rejected his findings.

Nor could the Reed board, however interested in the mosquito theory, accept records of the old doctor's experiments as proof, since Finlay's volunteers *all had had opportunity to contract the disease from sources other than his experimental mosquitoes.*

But if the mosquito was indeed the agent of the disease, how was it going to be proved? That was the question.

One thing was certain: Whatever was going to be done to stop the epidemic would have to be done in a hurry. The disease was making deadly strides among the American soldiers not only in Quemados and Havana, but also in Vedado, Matanzas, Santa Clara, Cienfuegos, Santiago, Guanajay and Pinar del Rio. At the latter post patients had been dying of what the post surgeon called "pernicious malaria." When Aristides Agramonte investigated he found that the disease was not malaria at all, but yellow fever. Dr. Reed hurried to Pinar del Rio, confirmed Agramonte's diagnosis and found a number of other cases in the hospital which the local post surgeon hadn't even recognized.

There was one special case at Pinar del Rio which gave the Major food for thought—and much hope. A soldier in trouble had on June 6 been thrown in the guardhouse. Over a month later, on July 12, he came down with yellow fever and died within six days. Since this soldier had not once been allowed out of the guardhouse he could not have caught the disease in town. There was another remarkable circumstance. Eight other prisoners occupied the same cell with the stricken soldier. None came down with yellow fever and one of them had even been sleeping in the dead soldier's bunk. To Major Reed this indicated that the unlucky prisoner could not have acquired yellow fever from infected food or contacts with the guards, for if he had the others would have been affected also. There seemed to be only one answer: since the soldier's bunk was near the window, a mosquito must have entered the bars of the cell, bitten the prisoner and flown out again. This of course could not be proved—it was merely circumstantial evidence. If yellow fever was indeed insect-borne, it would be necessary to conduct a thorough mosquito test.

This was begun but it was no simple matter because of the difficulty of raising mosquitoes under artificial conditions. The first eggs were obtained from old Dr. Finlay and were placed in the care of Board Member Jesse Lazear, who was in charge of the laboratory at Columbia Barracks. Under his supervision the insects were hatched in glass jars containing sweetened water and a slice of banana. Despite the best of care they proved very fragile and many died, whereupon more eggs had to be secured and hatched. Nor was that all. It was found that mosquitoes would not live long without feeding on human blood. Accordingly Lazear's assistant, Sergeant Neate, allowed the mosquitoes he had hatched to bite his hand every so often and drink their fill.

By August, 1900, the laboratory had a number of husky home-grown mosquitoes on hand and plans for the experiments had begun to take shape. But at this critical point the Surgeon-General ordered Major Reed to Washington to take part in preparing an important report on typhoid fever. On August 2nd the Major regretfully sailed for the United States.

6

A LONELY BUGLE FOR A TRUE MARTYR

Each age has its adventurers. For self-satisfaction, fame or money they walk Niagara Falls on a tight-rope, breast the currents of the English Channel, or pit their energies against an Alpine peak. The motives of these adventurers are essentially selfish, quite different from the motives of those who must gamble with their lives in war. The most unselfish, however, are those who deliberately offer to sacrifice their lives for the lives of others. The doctors on the Yellow Fever Board knew that the bite of a mosquito might bring death. But they considered their cause worth more than their lives.

Although Walter Reed was in Washington, D.C., Jesse Lazear went cautiously ahead with the Board's plans to try to infect its own members through the bites of mosquitoes. Lazear had been in Cuba since February, four months before the Board was organized, diligently studying secretions and tissues of yellow fever victims. He was thus able to verify that they had this disease, and not malaria or typhoid fever. However, neither he nor anyone else had been able to find the true yellow-fever germ or bacteria in the blood of those stricken with the disease. And with good reason: the agent responsible was the tiny virus. Viruses were unseen and unknown in 1900.

These investigations of course had nothing to

do with the mosquito program but they were a preparation for it. For if the Board knew a case of Yellow Jack when they saw one (even though they could not find the germ responsible for it) they could at least try to find out how it spread. And the mosquito seemed to be a likely suspect. Finlay, though sure of it, could not prove it. Lazear and Reed had come to be increasingly suspicious that it might be so. Now, thought Lazear, was the time to find out.

Accordingly he maneuvered his laboratory mosquitoes into test tubes and, by holding the open end of the tubes against the skin of yellow-fever patients, allowed the mosquitoes to drink their fill. Then in the heat of August he quietly applied the supposedly infected mosquitoes to the arms of eight volunteers including himself. Nothing whatever happened to any of them. This, thought Lazear, was strange but presently it occurred to him that the timing had been wrong. Perhaps mosquitoes might not be able to pass the disease along to others until as many as fourteen days had elapsed from the time they had first sucked the blood of yellow-fever patients.

On August 31st a mosquito which had bitten four persons ill with yellow fever for as long as twelve days previously, was applied by Lazear to the arm of Board Member James Carroll, the father of five small children. He light-heartedly laughed off the experiment, having, as yet, little of Lazear's faith in the mosquito theory. The next day, writing to Major Reed in Washington, Carroll explained what had been done. If there was any truth in the mosquito theory, he said, then he was about to have a first-class case of yellow fever.

Although he was up and about during the next two days, he was not well. Four days after he had been bitten he took to his bed. The following day he was found to be desperately ill with yellow fever and was carried off to the hospital. For ten days his life hung in the balance. On the thirteenth of September he struggled out of bed and slowly began to regain his strength.

Meanwhile another volunteer, 24-year-old Private Dean, who had been bitten by the same mosquito, also contracted the disease. His case was mild, however, and he recovered completely before Dr. Carroll left his bed.

Another brave man was not so lucky. On the eighteenth of September 34-year-old Dr. Lazear fell sick with yellow fever and died a week later in convulsions. During the first days of his illness he confided to his associates that he had been bitten by a mosquito while working in the hospital. After studying Lazear's notebook Dr. Reed later discovered that his unfortunate colleague had purposely applied one of his infected mosquitoes to his arm. He had done it secretly, for he could not bear to have his wife know that he was placing his life in jeopardy. When he became sick he therefore invented the story about being accidentally bitten.

As a civilian surgeon under contract Dr. Lazear was not entitled to military honors but Dr. Truby, the young commander of the post, saw to it that he received them. As the funeral procession wound across the bleak Quemados plateau, mournful music filled the air. At the grave, while Dr. Lazear's colleagues stood near with bowed heads, a bugler blew taps for a true martyr of humanity.

When news of Lazear's death reached him in Washington, Major Reed was grief-stricken. "He was a splendid brave fellow," he wrote later, "and I lament his loss more than words can tell, but his death was not in vain—his name will live in the history of those who have benefited humanity." The Major felt that in a way the tragedy was his fault, that perhaps it never would have happened if he had been permitted to remain in Cuba with his co-workers. But he had to content himself with the thought that the Surgeon-General would not have called him back to Washington unless he had been needed.

Great was the rejoicing when Major Reed returned to Columbia Barracks on October 4. His kind words and encouragement cheered even Dr. Carroll, still weak and depressed from his illness.

Now came a detailed review of the events during his absence. Dr. Reed sifted all of the records in the laboratory and every scrap of information regarding the cases of Carroll, Dean and Lazear. The more he studied them the surer he became that only the case of Dean would satisfy him for it was the only attempt so far to produce yellow fever under complete control, by the bite of an infected mosquito.

Lazear's own case could not be counted because no one would ever know just what circumstances had led to his illness. As for Dr. Carroll, he had visited both the bathing beach and the post-mortem room at Camp Columbia before he was taken sick, and the world would say that he had picked up the disease in one of these places. Major Reed's attention was thus drawn more closely to the case of Private Dean. He found that at the time Dean had been bitten the soldier was in the hospital for the treatment of another ailment. Reed realized that Lazear, in giving the test, should have received not only the soldier's permission but that of headquarters as well. If word got around that a soldier purposely infected with yellow fever was at large among 1,200 susceptible troops there might be unfortunate repercussions. Consequently the Major was careful to conceal Dean's identity in his reports by calling him XY.

However, Dean had suffered only a light case and was now completely well. What Walter Reed wanted to know was the answer to this question: Had the soldier left the Post to visit Quemados or downtown Havana prior to his last sickness? Careful checking revealed that after being bitten he had been discharged from the hospital and had gone directly to the Post, only to return to the hospital when Yellow Jack struck. In the intervening period he had not once left the Post.

Much heartened by this one strong case, the Major decided to prepare a report on the experiments conducted thus far. Day and night for eight days he feverishly labored over his findings, carefully weighing his words and interpreting Lazear's experiments—especially the three positive ones. When he finished his analysis there was absolutely no question in his mind that the mosquito was the deadly agent of Yellow Jack—and it was Dean's case that convinced him. It was time, he felt, to announce the results in the United States.

7

IN ANSWER TO A PRAYER

On October 13, 1900, Major Reed started out from Quemados for Havana in General Fitzhugh Lee's carriage. He greatly enjoyed this rig because it reminded him a little of the old days out West when he and Emilie rode in an Army wagon across the desert and through the canyons into a frontier country filled with adventures.

At this moment he was in the midst of the greatest adventure of his life, but there was nothing carefree or gay about it. It was an adventure with death. In Havana Yellow Jack had even struck down the staff of the American Governor-General, whom he was on his way to see. First Captain Cartwright had died, then Major Peterson. On the way to Peterson's funeral Captain Page had fallen ill and within 48 hours he died. So thorough was the course of the fever in its grim campaign against the staff at headquarters that it removed forty-eight civilian employees from their desks and left only two men at the officers' mess. They daily expected to join those who had gone. As in old England, it had become the custom at mealtime to drink to the departed and the about-to-depart with the toast: "To those who have already gone, and here's to the next to go."

Naturally, Leonard Wood, the American commanding general in Cuba and himself a doctor, had viewed Reed's experiments with the greatest hope.

It was as a fellow physician that the General greeted Walter Reed. Major Kean, who was present during this conference, never forgot the grave expressions on the faces of the two men at this dramatic moment in the history of medicine. They stood at a window of the palace at Havana, looking out on the Plaza de Armas, and beyond to the blue waters of the harbor. Reed, with the clarity and force of speech so characteristic of him, told his story while General Wood earnestly listened.

"General," said Reed, "we are in a desperate way. I think we must extend our program and make it absolutely foolproof by conducting it at an experimental camp under complete control."

"I want to help in every possible way, Major."

"I should like," Reed declared, "to move our experiments away from Columbia Barracks. We need to establish a yellow fever camp away from the Post. If we don't do this we can never convince the doubting Thomases that those who contract yellow fever from our mosquitoes did not pick up the disease at the Post, in Quemados, or some other place. I should like your permission to construct the camp in a sunny, open location a mile away from Quemados on the farm of Dr. Ignacio Rojas. Tents will be adequate for most purposes, but we are going to need two wooden buildings so tightly constructed and screened that our mosquitoes cannot get out and the outside mosquitoes cannot get in."

"And strictly quarantine your volunteers in the camp," added the General.

"Exactly. Also, if we are to establish our claims we must have a convincing percentage of cases. That means not just three or four volunteers, but many."

"Such a program will cause criticism in the United States," the General warned, "for what you will be doing is using human beings as guinea pigs."

"That is right," said the Major. "But from now on volunteers will be made grimly aware of what might happen to them. No pressure will be brought to bear. I do think that in order to obtain as many as we shall need we ought to offer them bonuses. They are risking their lives. But volunteers we must have if we are to conduct our program!" In broad outline he now described how the experiments were to be conducted. When he had finished, the General pledged $10,000 for the new program.

"And if that is not enough," he promised, "I will give you ten thousand dollars more. This is certainly of vastly greater importance to Cuba than the police force, which has been given a large sum for the catching of a few rogues. Be certain to take no men who are not sound in mind and body and of legal age according to Spanish law."

The conference having ended, the General sent Reed to the Quartermaster to order the equipment he needed. Thus plans went forward that day to build Camp Lazear on an isolated Cuban farm.

Having received General Wood's permission

to deliver an address in the United States on the current findings of the Yellow Fever Board, the Major left the next day for Minneapolis, where the Public Health Association was meeting. The reading of his report, strongly suggesting that the mosquito was responsible for yellow fever, was greeted with silence on the part of some doctors and scathing criticism on the part of others. On November 2nd, 1900, the enormously influential editorial pages of the *Washington Post* took up the cry: "Of all the silly and nonsensical rigmarole about yellow fever that has yet found its way into print—and there has been enough of it to load a fleet—the silliest beyond compare is to be found in the mosquito hypothesis. . . ."

While Walter Reed had not claimed that the evidence he had gathered was final, he had hoped for a more fair-minded response. Much discouraged, he returned to Columbia Barracks determined to wring from his experiments results so convincing that the doubting Thomases would have to eat their words. Yet even greater opposition descended upon him when he publicly proposed to use Spanish volunteers for his experiments. Black headlines in the Spanish newspapers shrieked: "HORRIBLE BUT TRUE—MURDER!"

But the Yellow Fever Board went unflinchingly ahead and in mid-November, 1900, Camp Lazear was ready with its complement of sixteen persons. The two buildings erected by the Army Engineers were called, respectively, Building Number 1 or the Infected Clothing Building, and Building Number 2, the Infected Mosquito Building. The mosquito building, carefully protected by fine screening, was designed to draw in plenty of fresh air. A screened partition across the interior divided it into two rooms. The idea of the partition was to separate volunteers who would be bitten by infected mosquitoes from the volunteers placed on the side where no mosquitoes could enter. The men on the "safe" side of the partition would not, if the theory was sound, get yellow fever.

The Infected Clothing Building, which was situated across a small valley eighty yards from its neighbor, was poorly ventilated—purposely so. The plan was to keep mosquitoes entirely out of this building. Volunteers were to be placed in it surrounded by every possible article that previously had been used by yellow fever patients—sheets, blankets, clothing, eating and drinking utensils. If it was possible to catch Yellow Jack in this way, Walter Reed would soon know. If not, the long-held "fomites" theory would soon be exploded.

One minor catastrophe delayed the start of the experiments. In mid-November a severe storm visited Cuba and blew the mosquitoes out to sea. In the accompanying 62-degree cold, most of the laboratory mosquitoes died. Major Reed was afraid that it would be impossible to find any more and consequently a busy search for mosquito eggs was begun. A fine supply was at last found in water at the bottom of discarded cans at the Post dump. These were taken to the laboratory where the experienced Sergeant Neate promptly hatched and exposed them to yellow fever patients. In this way the mosquito famine soon ended.

At this time Dr. Carroll, who had just returned from sick-leave in the United States, was helping with the mosquito program at Columbia Barracks. He was still not well enough to stand the rigors of life at the tent colony. Actually, as the experiments began, each of the staff doctors— Agramonte, Truby, Cooke, and Ames—had vital duties at the old or new camps. Although the atmosphere was electric with plans for the great events about to take place, the enlisted men adjusted themselves quite casually to their new duties.

Aware that he would be spending many hours at the tent colony, Major Reed had brought with him a packing box full of literature on yellow fever. He was particularly interested in what Dr. Henry R. Carter (one of the foremost students on yellow fever) had to say about an epidemic at Orwood and Taylor, Mississippi in 1898. Carter also was suspicious of the mosquito and had speculated about "incubation," yet this puzzling matter remained unsolved. At just what point in his disease could a yellow fever patient pass the germs of his infection on to a mosquito? And just how many days or weeks had to elapse before the mosquito was capable of infecting another individual? Lazear's experiments had confirmed to Reed what Carter had suggested—that a two-weeks' incubation period was necessary in the mosquito.

The whole program depended upon volunteers, and the members of the Yellow Fever Board could only hope that they would obtain some among the soldiers. Their duty lay in risking their lives in combat, not in tempting fate by purposely contracting a vicious disease. Still, there might be some among them who would decide that a challenge in the field of medicine offered no greater odds than a challenge on the field of combat. And while no value in dollars could be placed upon a human life, the Board made it known that a volunteer would receive $500.00 as a token reward for his risk.

One morning Assistant Surgeon Roger Ames chanced to meet John J. Moran, the young steward of the Post, and asked if he had heard about the reward. Moran, whose ambition was to become a doctor, replied that he had.

"There's a nice chance, Johnny, for you to bolster your slim educational fund," Dr. Ames suggested.

Moran agreed he could use the money and told Dr. Ames that he would sleep over it. That evening he brought up the subject with his roommate, Private John R. Kissinger of the hospital corps. Five hundred dollars, Moran said, would be of great help to a man like himself who expected to study medicine for four years.

"Still," Moran went on, "I somehow don't like the idea of accepting the money. If I went under, I wouldn't want an epitaph that read:

HERE LIE THE REMAINS OF JOHNNY MORAN

who lost his life in a good cause and spoiled it by accepting a reward of $500!

"I don't think you'd spoil anything by accepting that amount," said Kissinger. "There isn't enough money in Cuba to pay anyone for having Yellow Jack."

"This may sound a little too pure," replied Moran, "but if I volunteered for nothing I would be starting off my medical career with a noble act to my credit. It would be more satisfying to my self-respect."

"If you volunteer," Kissinger declared, "you may not have *any* career to worry about."

They laughed as they put out the oil lamp, climbed into their bunks and tried to go to sleep, but they could not put the matter out of their minds.

"John," Kissinger said not long before daybreak, "I can tell that you've decided to volunteer. I'm with you. And no five hundred dollars!"

"You're not serious!" said Moran.

"Yes, I am," replied Kissinger. "I've been thinking about it for several days. My mind was almost made up before you mentioned the subject."

"Great!" exclaimed Moran. "We'll volunteer together. But just because I'm not accepting the reward there's no reason you shouldn't."

"No reason," replied Kissinger sleepily, "but I'm not accepting it. You can't spend five hundred dollars in Heaven!"

The next morning the two young men appeared in Major Reed's office.

"Sir," Moran stated, "Kissinger and I have decided to volunteer for the mosquito test."

Walter Reed was greatly moved and could not for the moment find words to express his feelings. "I hope," he said at last, "that you have given a good deal of thought to this. It is a most serious decision."

"Sir," replied Moran, "we have been in Cuba for some time and know how terrible yellow fever is, but we would like to take the test just the same."

"Very well," replied the Major, "but I want you to understand that it is beyond the call of duty."

"We understand, Sir. Dr. Ames told us that volunteers are to receive five hundred dollars. But we are volunteering in the interests of medical science and will not accept any money. If any money is to be paid we cannot volunteer."

For a few moments Major Reed could merely look from one of these soldiers to the other. "I am proud," he said at last, "to accept your brave offer." He later wrote that "in my opinion this exhibition of moral courage has never been surpassed in the annals of the Army of the United States."

Moran and Kissinger were required to take very stiff physical examinations. Major Reed wanted to be sure that they were in prime physical condition, for if they were and they contracted yellow fever their chances for recovery would be that much better. He also advised them that they could select any doctor and nurse in Cuba to care for them. They chose Post Surgeon Ames and an Army graduate nurse named Mrs. Gillan.

The news that these two soldiers were about to take the mosquito test spread quickly through the small camp. Others followed their example, so that the Yellow Fever Board soon had a full quota of volunteers. These included Spaniards, each of whom was to be paid a reward.

Toward the end of November Camp Lazear was tense with excitement and apprehension. Infected mosquitoes, brought from the laboratory at Columbia Barracks, were put to work. They quickly bit Moran and Kissinger and the other subjects once, and some of them twice. But as the days passed the volunteers remained well.

To the Major this was puzzling, for infinite pains had been taken to be sure that conditions were exactly right. Also, enough time had elapsed since the "birds" (as the doctors called the mosquitoes) had first fed on yellow fever patients. Moran and Kissinger actually were discouraged. The fact that Yellow Jack did not strike at least one of them was an anticlimax after their solemn preparation. Reed finally decided that the cold weather had made it impossible for the mosquitoes to convey the disease.

In the third week of quarantine at Camp Lazear the weather turned warmer and Major Reed renewed the experiments. Moran and Kissinger were bitten again, as were three of the Spaniards who had volunteered. Three and a half days later—on

December 9—Kissinger was seized with a chill. Severe headache and backache followed, and the next day his temperature rose to 102.2 degrees.

On the morning of December 10 a group of Havana doctors arrived at Camp Lazear to see

Kissinger. None of them (except Dr. Finlay) were believers in the mosquito theory, but all were experts in diagnosing yellow fever. Old Dr. Finlay, originator of the mosquito theory, announced his verdict: "Yellow fever." The others would make

no statement. Returning to view the patient again on the following day, however, Major William C. Gorgas of the United States Army Medical Corps, Department of Havana, said: "This case is so suspicious that had it occurred in Havana I would not have hesitated to send the patient to the yellow fever hospital." The others also had to admit that it looked as though Kissinger had yellow fever.

Such an admission on the part of doctors who had called the mosquito theory a "wild" one meant everything to Walter Reed and his program. The doctors inspecting Kissinger were the voices of Havana and, in a larger sense, the voices of the world. If they thought that there was something to the mosquito theory after all, the world would believe it too. For to admit that Kissinger was ill with yellow fever was to admit that the mosquito had conveyed the disease—there was virtually no other possibility. The Havana experts well knew that Kissinger had been in quarantine and could not have caught the disease elsewhere. They knew that he had become ill three and a half days after being bitten.

But Kissinger was not the only exhibit Major Reed had in store for the Havana doctors. There was the Infected Clothing House. In this foul-smelling building three volunteers—Dr. Cooke and Privates Folk and Jernegan—had been living for almost two weeks. They were using sheets, pillow-cases and blankets which had been brought straight from the death-beds of yellow fever patients. They were wearing soiled nightshirts. The stench from these articles was terrible, for there was no venti-lation in the room. Yet all three men were enjoy-ing excellent health. What did the Havana doctors think of their "fomites" theory now?

Much wiser for their tour, the experts returned to Havana. Whatever doubts they still might have had were erased by a quick succession of events back at the camp. Three Spanish volunteers who had been bitten shortly after Kissinger came down with the disease. No one was more surprised than the Spanish patients themselves, for they had told Reed that mosquitoes were as harmless as the little flies that buzzed about their tables. In the imaginations of the other Spaniards about to take the test, mosquitoes now began to assume the size of buzzards. Ignoring promised rewards, some of them fled the camp.

The lowly mosquito was now accorded the respect of all. The laboratory where the insects were kept obviously was as dangerous as if it stored nitro-glycerin. And when an infected *Aedes* escaped from her glass jar, Sergeant Neate pursued her relentlessly around the room until he bagged her and safely returned her to her jar.

On one occasion a group of physicians came from other countries to see what Major Reed was doing. They believed in "fomites" and a tour through the mosquito room did little to convince them of the insect theory. Even so, when one of the mosquitoes accidentally escaped from her glass jar during the demonstration, all of the dignified doctors turned white, made a hasty about-face and charged for the exit. So hurried were they in their flight that they broke down the screen door!

Of the tests that followed during succeeding days, that of Private Moran was of great importance, for he had twice taken the mosquito test and each time failed to come down with the disease. Now another attempt would be made. Accordingly, at noon on December 21, Moran, fresh from a bath, entered the mosquito room, lay down on the bed and was bitten seven times in thirty minutes by mosquitoes which had all fed on victims of yellow fever from five to twenty-five days previously. Moran reëntered the room at 4:30 the same day and was bitten five more times. The following day three more mosquitoes fed upon him.

During the next three days Moran felt very fit and on Christmas morning was beginning to wonder whether he was going to fail what Major Reed called his "master test." In fact, Moran was quite annoyed that Kissinger, by this time completely well, had beaten him to a case of Yellow Jack. There was one consolation, though—he would win his bet with Warren Jernegan. The latter, a volunteer for the "infected bedding and clothing" test, had bet Moran two five-dollar gold pieces that he would not eat Christmas dinner at Camp Lazear. Christmas dinner was only three hours away and he was still feeling fine. In the meantime, he had enjoyed a good night's sleep and a big breakfast.

At ten o'clock in the morning, in the office tent where he helped with the paper work, Moran suddenly felt a flushing sensation in his face and head. He took his own temperature and found it to be 100.4, nearly two degrees above normal. Could it be that he had Yellow Jack after all? At noon he was feeling quite sick and he found that his temperature had risen another degree. Never mind! He was going to win the bet. Making his way rather shakily to the mess tent, he greeted his comrades with a smile and served himself a helping of turkey, cranberry sauce and plum pudding. Although his appetite was delicate, he could have eaten more than he did. But Major Reed had said that it was most important for a yellow fever victim not to eat. So Moran ate just enough to keep the others from suspecting anything. As for Jernegan, he was so busy with his mountainous helping of turkey that he paid little attention to Moran.

"Warren," said Moran when the meal was over, "how about those two five-dollar gold pieces?"

"Guess you win," and Jernegan laughed. "You can't kill an Irishman anyway!"

Happily pocketing the shining yellow coins, Moran declared: "You lose and win at the same time."

Jernegan looked at him tensely and with great concern. "You don't mean to tell me that you have it, Johnny?"

Moran nodded.

Within two seconds silence overtook the boisterous chatter in the tent.

Moran was the first to find his voice again. "I may be out of circulation for a few days," he said, smiling wanly, "but I'll be back for some cold turkey—if you haven't eaten it all." He left the tent in a shower of good wishes, preferring to return to the office tent alone. There he heavily threw himself down on the cot. And there he stayed, except to take and record his temperature which was soon over 103.

At 3:00 P.M. Major Reed came in.

"Merry Christmas, Moran," he said. "Anything new?"

From his cot Moran pointed to the temperature chart on the Major's field desk. Reed glanced at it and as he turned to Moran his face lighted up in a smile broader than if he had been made a general. "Moran!" he exclaimed. "This is one of the happiest days of my life!" But in a moment he became the God-fearing medical scientist that he was.

Counseling his patient not to worry, he rushed out of the tent and in a twinkling had procured the mule-drawn Army ambulance from Camp Columbia. Soon the star patient was on his way to the post hospital, with Major Reed directly behind in another wagon.

As the hours of Christmas night passed, Yellow Jack unleashed all its fury on Moran, now so sick that he did not know or care what was going on around or within him. Dully he remembered being packed in ice in a portable bathtub, and the soft voice of his nurse urging him not to allow the cracked ice she offered to melt in his mouth, but to swallow it. His whole body seemed to be on fire. He tried but could not respond to the voice of Dr. Ames, in whose care he had been placed. As the clock ticked off the dragging seconds of the night the anxious figures by his bedside tirelessly waged war with his soaring temperature.

In the morning Moran was aware that someone was nudging him. Trying hard to think and to see, he gradually became aware that a middle-aged officer with an anxious look in his eyes was speaking to him. He simply could not respond until it dawned upon him that it was Major Reed.

"Are you in pain, boy?" Major Reed asked.

"Yes, sir," replied the weak voice.

"Try to localize the pains for me, will you?"

What did he mean by localize? Oh yes, tell where the pains were. "I am just one mass of pain."

"Don't you feel like groaning? Sometimes groaning gives relief and no one will mind. Why don't you try it?"

Scarcely above a whisper Moran replied: "I hoped to take it with as little fuss as possible. . . ." Then he drifted off into semi-delirium.

For several days Moran's claim on life was a very fragile one; for a week he ate or drank nothing and his weight dropped more than thirty pounds. But on the eighth day he took a teaspoonful of milk and improved rapidly thereafter. The care he received from Dr. Ames partly accounted for his complete recovery, as in the case of the other volunteers, but there seemed also to have been some special dispensation from Heaven.

Not a life lost! The doubting Havana doctors *had* to accept the mosquito theory now. The tests were so conclusive that there was simply no other possibility. Beyond the marvelous plan itself, the world could look for the success of the experiments to the volunteers and to the doctors—dead and alive—who had made it possible.

Private Warren Jernegan had first volunteered to live in the Infected Clothing Building, which he did for twenty days. Failing to catch yellow fever there, he took the mosquito test. When this too failed, he volunteered for the blood-inoculation test to prove whether it was possible to transmit the disease by directly injecting the blood of a yellow fever patient into the system of another person. In this way Yellow Jack at last struck Jernegan, and he was satisfied.

Major Reed himself had on several occasions

expressed his willingness to take the test but was advised against doing so by his fellow doctors. They told him, quite rightly, that his health was too vital to the experiment. In all, fourteen American and Spanish volunteers developed yellow fever at Camp Lazear between November 20 and February 10. The names of the nine American volunteers, together with those of the Yellow Fever Board members, were eventually inscribed on the Roll of Honor of the Congress of the United States. The names of the Spanish volunteers appear in the memorial at Camp Lazear. Of the discoveries there it has been said that they were worth more than the cost of the whole Spanish-American War, including lives lost and money expended.

"I suppose that old Dr. Finlay will be delighted beyond bounds," Walter Reed unselfishly wrote his wife toward midnight, December 31, 1900, "as he will see his theory at last fully vindicated.

. . . The prayer that has been mine for twenty years, that I might be permitted to do something to alleviate human suffering, has been granted! . . . Hark, there go the twenty-four buglers in concert, all sounding 'taps' for the old year."

8

GOOD NEWS FROM HAVANA

If all the mosquitoes in the world could be brought together, how high a pile would they make—as high as the Washington monument? Who knows? Who cares! We will never get the best of them. Through the bitter winters of the north and in the steaming heat of the jungles, they persist in prodigious numbers.

Among almost 800 varieties is the *Anopheles*, carrier of malaria fever. The yellow fever mosquito, *Aedes aegypti*, with its silvery body stripes and zebra-striped legs, is found in the United States and Europe, Africa, South and Central America, India—in all tropical, sub-tropical and even temperate zones. Since it likes villages and cities, it is known as a domestic insect. It breeds in puddles, rain barrels or stopped-up roof gutters, cisterns, fire buckets, jugs and old tin cans—in anything near a house where fresh water collects. Here at night, after a meal of human blood, the female lays her jet-black eggs. Clustering in groups of 20 to 75, they will hatch even if they have dried out or frozen. The larval period lasts about a week, and after two days in the pupa stage the tiny wiggler develops into a full-fledged mosquito. *Aedes* does not fly far, seeks shelter in a wind and likes to live its entire life inside a house.

The male of *Aedes aegypti* does not bite at all. The female bites when she has become impregnated, and then only when the temperature is above 62 degrees. She is canny, for she almost never bites the top of the hand where she can be slapped, but strikes the ankle, under-wrist, or some such vulnerable place. After the female has bitten a victim of yellow fever, about two weeks must elapse before she can pass the disease on to another person. After that she may continue to convey the disease for as long as two months.

Now that a distinguished group of doctors and volunteers had proved that *Aedes* was the enemy, the new problem was: what weapons could be found to combat an epidemic like the one now raging in Cuba? Doctors Reed and L. O. Howard had determined that the mosquitoes had to be annihilated, or at least controlled, and had carefully outlined methods for doing so. While it was an enormous task—something like trying to shoot down a squadron of bombers with a BB gun—all-out warfare on *A. aegypti* was the only way of keeping Yellow Jack in bounds.

Major Kean drew up detailed plans and wrote the first orders in the anti-mosquito campaign. These were carried out by William C. Gorgas, a slim energetic major in the Medical Corps. Early in the Spanish-American War Gorgas had been sent to Cuba as Sanitation Officer, a position of great trust, for the prevention of many diseases depended upon the cleanliness of areas where troops were quartered. Since it was then thought that yellow fever was also caused by filth, Dr. Gorgas announced his intention of cleaning up the city of Havana.

"Let me give it a good scouring and a bath," he declared, "and yellow fever and other diseases will disappear." With marvelous energy he and his men set to work removing dead cats, garbage and debris from the streets, burning rubbish, draining gutters, installing plumbing in stores, hotels and homes, pouring cement floors in stables. He gave Havana such a face-lifting that toward the end of the war on the mosquitoes it did not look like the same place.

Unhappily, however, yellow fever did not diminish in virulence. On the contrary, it gained. Gorgas did not even faintly suspect the reason: the flood of immigrants sweeping into Havana. Most of the native people were immune to Yellow Jack, having lived with it for so many generations. Not so the newcomers, who were quickly attacked by the city's swarms of mosquitoes. Indeed, the insects struck hardest in the very sections of the city that Major Gorgas had cleaned the most thoroughly. The reason they did, of course, was that most of the immigrants had chosen to live there in those sections. The epidemic passed over the native immunes who inhabited the less cleanly sections of the city.

This defeat called for even greater effort on the part of Gorgas and his clean-up squads. The sweeping, scrubbing and fumigating were now carried into the farthest corners of Havana. Still to no avail. The death notices in the newspapers daily grew bigger and blacker.

Havana's aging Doctor Finlay told Gorgas that he was going about it in the wrong way. The mosquito was to blame, Finlay insisted, and cleaning up garbage would not help a whit. But Gorgas paid no attention.

As a matter of fact, when Walter Reed began his experiments, Gorgas had no faith in the insect theory. But when Reed finally assembled his evidence against the mosquito, the Sanitary Officer acknowledged the errors of his own thinking.

"If it is the mosquito," he declared, "I am going to get rid of the mosquito."

Major Kean's original orders had called for all officers and men to sleep under netting until the mosquito could be eliminated. Then destruction of mosquito larvae by the use of petroleum was begun. Fire buckets, water barrels, cisterns and other vessels that could not be emptied were to be covered once a month with a thin coating of kerosene. So long as drinking water was drawn from the bottom of such containers, its quality was not hurt at all. At the same time, the film of kerosene on the surface made it impossible for the mosquito wigglers to reach the surface of the water for oxygen, and thus they were destroyed.

In the spring and summer of 1901 Gorgas traded his clean-up squads for mosquito brigades, whose headquarters became the American Sanitary Administration. In a building on the Havana waterfront Gorgas and his staff compiled records of every house in Havana and every family that made up the city's population of 300,000. Each home was represented by a large piece of white cardboard on which Gorgas pinpointed the location of every jug, cistern, tank or barrel. This information made it much easier for his mosquito brigades to know what they had to do on their monthly inspections. Entering a home, they would go immediately to the water vessels indicated on their chart and pour an ounce or so of kerosene in them. Their hope was that by doing this thoroughly in every part of the city, the frustrated mosquitoes would have no place to lay their eggs, and even if they did lay them the wigglers would not live.

The trouble was that the kerosene often evaporated before the inspectors could get around on their next visit. Meanwhile a new army of mosquitoes would have emerged and taken wing. Gorgas therefore adopted a second measure. His inspectors tightly boarded up the tops of all large receptacles, leaving a small screen-covered hole which would admit rainwater but not mosquitoes.

But that was only part of the job. While the big receptacles were not so hard to find and take care of, each householder had any number of small pots, pans or pitchers lying around which served as excellent traps for rainwater and thus were first-class mosquito factories. Gorgas's squads had therefore to learn and record the whereabouts of the pots, pans and pitchers owned by the 300,000 people of Havana. Great numbers of citizens regarded the brigades as a joke and a nuisance. They would do everything they could to foil the authorities despite a fine of ten dollars levied upon them by the city if they willfully allowed mosquitoes to breed on their premises.

No one wants inspectors trooping through his house, and if it had not been for Major Gorgas's good humor and patience his whole program might have collapsed. As it was, he gradually educated the people, rich and poor, to the importance of helping the inspectors. A twelve- or fourteen-hour working day meant nothing to him and, after he had left his office, he was likely to be found poking around some back alley of the city looking for concealed water receptacles. His face became so familiar in Havana that when Spanish housewives saw him coming they would call out good-naturedly: "No mosquitoes here, Señor!"

The mosquitoes proved far more contrary in

their struggle for survival than anyone had supposed. On one occasion recalled by Marie Gorgas in a biography of her husband, a Havana doctor stormed into Gorgas's office one morning and complained: "Your whole plan's a failure! I have emptied every last water vessel in my house and I still have mosquitoes. The house is full of them."

"Let me send one of my inspectors over," said Gorgas, "and we will try to solve the mystery." In searching the physician's house the inspector was also baffled. He decided to re-inspect every inch of the place. In so doing, he came across a box of books. Now there was nothing suspicious about that, but as a matter of routine Gorgas removed the books. At the bottom of the box was an old water-filled paint pail swarming with wigglers! How the female mosquitoes were able to find their way down through the books, and how the newly-hatched mosquitoes managed to find their way up through them, was a conundrum. The incident illustrated the perseverance of this insect and the immense problem facing those whose job was to rid Havana of it.

One would be justified in thinking that this task alone was enough to keep two thousand men busy. But Gorgas's hard-working mosquito brigades were also responsible for a different part of the program. As soon as they learned of a case of yellow fever, they fumigated every room of the infected home and swept up the dead mosquitoes. They would then place the patient in a room which they had screened so carefully that no outside mosquitoes could get in to bite the patient and thus become infected in turn. Guards were placed at the doors of the house to keep out all unauthorized persons. In this way there was practically no chance for the disease to escape the confines of the house.

Although Gorgas worried over certain cases too mild to be detected but still capable of spreading the contagion, he hoped that his war on the insects themselves would prevent the start of an epidemic from such cases.

Week by week and month by month his inspectors reported fewer and fewer mosquitoes and, almost as if by magic, fewer and fewer cases of Yellow Jack. By early fall it was clear to all that the work of the mosquito-brigades had borne results that were perfectly spectacular. For 150 years there had never been a day in Havana when the specter of Yellow Jack had not been seen in the streets. During that time there were many years when thousands of victims had died of the disease; in luckier years the figure still ran into the hundreds.

The Gorgas squads started work in March, 1901. In April, May and June there were no deaths from yellow fever. There was one in July, there were two in August and two in September. *During the following nine months there were none.*

"The news from Havana is simply delightful,"

wrote Walter Reed from Washington. "That you have suceeded in throttling the epidemic appears beyond question and it is to your everlasting credit. A man of less discretion, enthusiasm and energy would have made a fiasco of it."

"Yours was the guiding hand in the whole matter," replied Gorgas. "I am very happy to serve in the more humble role of putting your discovery into practice."

WALTER
REED
1851·1902

9

IN MEMORY OF THE CONQUEROR

A certain fickleness which might be called the band-wagon trait is common to most of us. Instead of trusting our own better instincts we join the parade of popular sentiment. This was never better displayed than in the reaction to the discoveries about yellow fever. Led by a corps of skeptical physicians, the public at large shrugged off the experiments in Cuba and the United States and were inclined to dismiss Walter Reed as an eccentric. But they almost smothered him with praise when he finally proved old Dr. Finlay's theories.

In December, 1900, sixty Havana doctors, many of whom had been the loudest critics of Finlay and Reed, gave the former an elegant banquet at the Delmonico Restaurant in Havana. The after-dinner praise that engulfed Finlay and Reed was as heavy as the cigar smoke that filled the banquet hall. Lavish praise, too, came from the members of the Pan-American Congress whom Reed addressed at their meeting in Havana the following February. And yet if some of his volunteers had died he would have been pilloried by these same people, his experiments might have been cut off, and his name would have been one that the Army Medical Corps would have been glad to forget. Fortunately Post Surgeon Ames's infinite care of the patients and a kind Providence decreed otherwise. Finlay and Reed were the men of the hour, doctors who had made one of the greatest medical discoveries of the century.

When he returned to Washington, D.C. in February, 1901, Walter Reed took up his former duties as a professor of bacteriology in the Army Medical School and also at the Columbian University. He was a favorite with his students, for he conveyed an enthusiasm for his subject that is the mark of great teachers. It was said that he liked especially to lead his pupils along the paths of new principles and new truths. They "were not always the well-traveled avenues of old lines of thought but, on the contrary, entirely new, strange and perhaps lonely ways, far out on the prairies of investigation. . . ."

It was in recognition of such laborious journeys into the unknown that President Eliot of Harvard University conferred upon Dr. Reed an honorary degree of Master of Arts with the citation: "Walter Reed, graduate of the University of Virginia, the Army surgeon who planned and directed in Cuba the experiments which have given man control over that fearful scourge, yellow fever."

Their son and daughter having grown up—Walter Lawrence was now a 24-year-old lieutenant in the Army—Dr. Reed and his wife found new leisure at their country cottage at Blue Ridge Summit, Pennsylvania. The doctor needed such rest, for his labors seemed to have sapped his strength. In October, 1902, as he again took up his teaching after his return from Blue Ridge Summit, he showed signs of being ill. When he came home from a day's work his face would be gray and lined. One night, on his way to give a lecture, he said to his wife: "I cannot realize that I ever delivered this lecture. It is utterly beyond my mental capacity now." Among his associates he made a good show of health and energy, but in November he confided to his faithful, longtime messenger at the Medical Museum: "Beechner, I am a very sick man."

On Wednesday, November 12, he was stricken with indigestion and remained in bed until noon the next day. Then he struggled into his clothes and went out, still suffering from pain in his abdomen. The following day he told his friend, Major Borden, that he thought he had appendicitis. Borden confirmed this diagnosis and sent him to the hospital where for the next day or so he showed much improvement. But on Sunday the pain returned, his temperature rose and Dr. Borden decided to operate the next morning. In those days removal of the appendix was neither easy nor common.

Assisting Dr. Borden at the operation was Walter Reed's friend and fellow-worker, Lt. Truby, who had been in charge of the hospital at Columbia Barracks when the Reed Board was carrying on its experiments. Major Kean, another friend and colleague, was looking on.

"Kean," said Dr. Reed, "I am not afraid of the knife, but if anything should happen to me, I am leaving my wife and daughter so little." Then, as he slipped under ether, Kean heard him whisper: "So little . . . so little."

The operation was a complicated one, as the appendix and surrounding area were badly inflamed. Peritonitis developed and, because there was little in those days that could be done to treat it, Kean and the other doctors lost all hope of saving the life of Walter Reed. He hung on for five days and died about two o'clock on the morning of November 23. A great concourse of people, including the Secretary of War and other high-ranking officers of the government, were present at his funeral in St. Thomas Church, Washington, D.C. He received a soldier's burial in Arlington.

After his death, his friends established the Walter Reed Memorial Association to provide for the care of Emilie Reed and her daughter. The fund of $25,000 was subscribed, it is said, by John D. Rockefeller.

10

A FLOWER IN THEIR BUTTONHOLES

Yellow Jack continued to plague mankind. The disease had been wiped out in Cuba, but this was merely a pin-point in *Aedes aegypti's* vast domain. Every so often the pestholes of South and Central America, where yellow fever flourished the year around, gave rise to epidemics in the United

States. The people along the northern shores of the Gulf of Mexico felt as if they were living at the foot of a volcano.

Aedes showed great ingenuity in spreading yellow fever. She would fly through the porthole of a ship docked at a South or Central American port and bite one of the crew members. The sailor would fall sick soon after setting sail, or upon reaching the new port—New Orleans, Charleston or New York. Northern mosquitoes now bit him and spread the infection to others so that soon a new epidemic raged.

Naturally it took some time for the various governments to set up regulations for the fumigation of ships leaving the yellow fever zone, and for the quarantining of passengers. Until these steps were taken, the only thing that could be done was to control the epidemic wherever it broke out. This was not hard to do if the people cooperated, but if they did not it was very difficult. When Yellow Jack struck Laredo, Texas, in 1903, great numbers of poor people in the town hid their sick, concealed their water barrels, and in some cases threatened to kill the inspectors. They were convinced that the medical men, in pouring kerosene in their water barrels, were trying to poison them all and end the epidemic that way! While the authorities could and did declare martial law and enforce their program, they realized this was not the best method in the long run. Educating the people as to the cause of yellow fever, they felt, was the only real solution to the problem.

Fortunately by 1905 the public at large had become well enough acquainted with the Reed and Gorgas methods of fighting mosquitoes to accept them. Accordingly, when yellow fever struck New Orleans in July, the citizens rallied as if they were taking part in a crusade. The doctors joined hands and formed "flying squadrons"; the city was organized into wards, and the state into church parishes. As the death rate mounted, thousands of placards appeared in the streets bearing the words:

**WEAR A SMILE ON YOUR FACE
AND A
FLOWER IN YOUR BUTTONHOLE**

Instead of shrinking fearfully into their homes, the citizens reported to the Marine Hospital Service for duty and thousands were soon at work in every quarter of the city's 44 square miles. They disinfected fifty-five thousand rooms, burned more than 200 tons of sulphur and pyrethrum, and poured sixty thousand gallons of oil in cisterns and gutters.

As a result, only 452 died of yellow fever in a city of nearly a third of a million people, and most of these contracted the disease while the mosquito campaign was getting under way. Thus, the crusade was a marked success, for in previous years Yellow Jack had reaped a total of 28,626 lives in New Orleans alone. Had it not been for Finlay, Lazear, Reed, and the brave volunteers who worked with them, the summer of 1905 would have brought even greater tragedy to the old city on the Mississippi.

As it happened, there was never another yellow-fever summer in New Orleans or any other place in the United States. So well did the doctors repel the invader that people would have forgotten the disease were it not for a certain slice of land in the jungles of Central America.

It was not really land at all, but a sinkhole of swamp—steaming hot, dim and frightful. Beneath a tangle of foliage that blotted out the sun dwelt tropical creatures of all kinds—alligators, lizards, centipedes, snakes and scorpions.

This was the Isthmus of Panama—a forty-mile link between the Atlantic and Pacific oceans. Nations regarded the Isthmus as very desirable because it was a water gap that nearly joined the Atlantic and Pacific oceans. There was some land in the way and there were rocky hills, but men could remove these. They could cut down the jungles and wrest the swamps away from the alligators.

But they did not count on one foe here—the tiny mosquito.

11

THE BATTLE OF THE ISTHMUS

If the American public was unaware that Yellow
Jack had shattered French dreams of a canal link-
ing the oceans, William Gorgas did not doubt
it. *Aedes aegypti's* recent assault upon the French
was merely the climax of her long reign of terror
in Panama. Throughout history the Isthmus had

served as a forty-mile thoroughfare for great numbers of strangers—the Spanish on their way home with treasure, the tens of thousands of Americans en route to the California gold fields—all easy targets for clouds of tropical mosquitoes.

Ferdinand De Lesseps of the French canal company might have saved an army of lives and the honor of his country if he had only listened to the dire warning of Monsieur Le Blanc, a French resident of Panama: "If you try to build this canal, there will not be trees enough on the Isthmus to make crosses for the graves of your laborers."

Scarcely had De Lesseps and his thousands of men started work in 1881 when Yellow Jack again began to stalk the swampy jungle. Soon thirty or forty workmen were dying every day and it was said that funeral trains on the Panama Railroad were as common as those carrying living passengers and freight. Nevertheless, the attempt to build the canal was continued. France was a great country, labor was cheap and there were always replacements for the dead. But the replacements soon died also, as did the officers and crews of the ships that brought them.

Laborers, superintendents, engineers and directors—they all succumbed to yellow fever. Chief Engineer Jules Dingler was more fortunate. And as if to serve notice of his authority as Lord High Chamberlain of the canal, he built an enormous house on the Isthmus costing the canal company $150,000 and sent for his family. On their arrival from France, Dingler's wife, son, daughter and her fiancé were struck down by Yellow Jack. One after another they all perished until only the chief engineer was left. When he later returned to France, a tragic victim of pride and circumstance, about all that remained in Panama to show for his efforts was "Dingler's Folly," his ornate and costly house.

Because the canal company did not want anyone to know the price it was paying in human life during its eight years in the swamps of Panama, the total number of deaths will never be known. There were certainly no fewer than twenty thousand, and Yellow Jack and malaria would have raised this to a still more frightful total if workers had not fled from the Isthmus by the thousands. Gradually growing feebler, the efforts of the De Lesseps Company at length ceased altogether. The jungle foliage, nourished by torrential rains and by the tropical sun, hid the rusty steam shovels and the graves of the men who ran them.

When the United States Government announced its intention of building the Panama Canal, it was confident that the Army Engineers could cope with the massive problems of excavation. But what if the Medical Corps could not banish yellow fever and malaria? The startling success of William Gorgas in ridding Havana of disease had earned him the gratitude of the government and the confidence of the medical profession. It had been one thing, of course, to fight the mosquito in a city like Havana, but it would be quite another to do so in the dirty towns on the edge of the Panama jungle. Still, thought William Gorgas, the lessons Walter Reed had taught in Cuba must apply elsewhere as well, for the mosquito was the only agent that spread yellow fever. If it could be destroyed, then the disease must disappear also. Confident that he could wage a successful mosquito war on the Isthmus, William Gorgas received a new assignment as Chief Sanitation Officer of the Panama Canal.

Newly promoted to the rank of lieutenant colonel, he left for Egypt in 1902 to study the Suez Canal in order that he might become more familiar with the great problems ahead. These were not long in presenting themselves when in 1904 he began work in Panama with eight associates. The Canal Commission naïvely expected that without help this tiny group could deal effectively with the disease. Gorgas had some good men with him—doctors like Henry Carter, whose

research in yellow fever had been most valuable
to Walter Reed in conducting his experiments in
Cuba. But Gorgas well knew that he could not
accomplish much without a small regiment of
workers as well. The Canal Commissioners were
not impressed. Workers cost money and expenses
must be kept down. In fact, the Commissioners
would not even give Gorgas the sulphur, screening and other supplies that he sorely needed. Their
reasoning was that the Culebra Cut could not be
dug with mosquito netting. When he cabled for
help, the Commissioners advised him that cables
were expensive and that he should use the mails
in the future.

Deeply discouraged, Colonel Gorgas returned
to the United States where he became so ensnarled
in red tape that he almost decided to give up the
job. Admiral John Walker, head of the Canal
Commission, did not believe in Walter Reed's
theories. He declared that filth caused the disease.

The ports of Panama and Colon were filthy and Gorgas's job was to clean them up.

For hours on end Gorgas had patiently explained to the Admiral that he himself had been a disciple of the filth theory and that his first campaign to clean up Havana had had absolutely no effect. He described every step of Reed's experiments, and how knowledge of the mosquitoes' habits had been used to rid Havana of yellow fever. But the Admiral was not convinced. Gorgas then tried to enlist the help of the first governor of the Canal Zone, General George Davis. The General, however, was a kindly man whose thoughts were completely taken up with engineering problems. In a fatherly manner he told Gorgas: "A dollar spent on sanitation is like throwing it into the bay."

A lesser man would have found the odds against him too great. To Colonel Gorgas the job now became a crusade.

Determined to do the best he could with what he was given and what he might get by fighting, he returned to the jungles of the Isthmus and to the mud and slime of the filthy ports that bordered on the Atlantic and Pacific. Here he struggled—knowing that yellow fever was going to strike in the coming weeks and that he would be helpless to prevent it from spreading.

Like a man with his hands tied behind his back. William Gorgas waited for Panama's countless squads of mosquitoes to open fire against the shiploads of canal workmen arriving every week from the United States. They would die, many of them, because of the stupidity of the Canal commissioners. And he himself would be vilified because he was the chief medical officer of the Canal, and any epidemic would be blamed on him.

The headquarters of the American canal-building forces was a Panama City building that had formerly been occupied by the ill-fated De Lesseps Company. Unscreened for the most part and full of crannies through which mosquitoes could find their way to the three hundred young Americans now working within, the building was more dangerous than the heart of the jungle. In it the house-loving *Aedes* could find not only water receptacles (such as vessels for keeping copying brushes moist) where she could lay her eggs, but great numbers of human hostages to feed upon. Time and time again Gorgas's chief inspector, Mr. Le Prince, begged the architect who was reconstructing the building to put screens on the windows and plug the holes. And day after day the architect, quite as cold to the Sanitation Department as his superiors, ignored the request.

"You're off in the upper story," he told Le Prince.

"Supposing we have twenty deaths here. Who will be responsible?" asked Le Prince.

"I'll stand the responsibility," said the architect.

A month later yellow fever broke out in the

unscreened office of the architect. Yellow Jack's first victim was the architect himself.

Reports of other cases at first trickled and then streamed into Gorgas's headquarters and by early 1905 the epidemic had gained real momentum. So frightened were the laborers that they began to abandon their machines and tools. New recruits from the United States returned in the same ships in which they had come. The Canal's capable and much-liked chief engineer, John F. Wallace, who lived in perpetual fear of Yellow Jack and who had brought his own casket with him, resigned and returned to the United States. When twenty-two more cases broke out in the administration building and several officers died, panic seized the whole American establishment. Time was running backward to the tragic days of De Lesseps.

William Gorgas was the one man who could prevent history from repeating itself, if he was permitted to fight with more than his bare hands. Fortunately the local officers of the Canal at last began to pay attention to him. Wasting no time in telling them "I told you so," he now doubled and redoubled his efforts. The hour was late, yet with more help and materials he seemed cheerfully confident of stopping the epidemic.

Just as he had done in Havana he divided the towns of Colon and Panama into sectors and dispatched his men to oil the rain barrels and cisterns and to empty the thousands of water containers thick with mosquito larvae. Strangely enough one of the worst focal points of yellow fever was the clean, well-run Ancon Hospital, which had been built by the French. Patients who went there for the treatment of a minor ailment came down with yellow fever before they had left. Thus the hospital came to be regarded not as a protector of life, but as a place of death. Gorgas soon found out why. To protect the patients from the ants which infested most Panama buildings, the four legs of each hospital bed rested in jars of water. The drowned ants shared the jars with thousands of mosquito larvae. Each patient was thus only as far away from yellow fever as the legs of his bed. The Medical Corps removed the jars and screened the windows. So ended Ancon Hospital's own furious epidemics.

As soon as his inspectors got the upper hand in the house-to-house campaign, Gorgas used a new weapon to dispose of the remaining mosquitoes. At many places he had his men set out dishes of water sweetened with sugar. Deprived of her usual household haunts, the destitute *Aedes* found the sweet water exactly to her liking and deposited her eggs there. The inspectors then came around, emptied the dishes and destroyed the eggs, filled the traps again and the whole process was repeated. Through this clever deception, the mosquitoes unwittingly wiped themselves out.

12

"WE'LL SEE IT THROUGH"

The impatient Canal commissioners had little faith
in Gorgas's peculiar program, which took some
time to bear fruit. Nor did his popularity improve
when a pompous navy captain stepped into the
shower at a Panama hotel, turned on the water
and was plastered with tar-like oil which drained

down from Colonel Gorgas's mosquito-proof cistern on the roof!

In 1905, during the very months when his Sanitation Department succeeded in strangling the epidemic, Colonel Gorgas found himself on the verge of dismissal from his job. Ever since they took office, Admiral Walker and the other commissioners in Washington had been sniping at him for spending money on mosquitoes instead of cleaning up the towns on the Isthmus, and for failure to prevent the outbreak of the epidemic. Month after month they poured their grievances into the ears of Secretary of War William Howard Taft, until he decided that for the sake of harmony among the commissioners, Gorgas must go.

The Secretary was just at the point of acting when the American Medical Association sent one of its former presidents, Dr. Charles Reed, a noted surgeon (not related to Walter Reed), to Panama to learn the truth about conditions there. Reed remained on the Isthmus about three weeks, probing into every corner of William Gorgas's establishment. When he returned to the United States he wrote a report that was printed in nearly every newspaper in the country. In prose that was clear and dignified and at the same time scathing and contemptuous, he described in detail the sorry effects in Panama of the commissioners' stupidity. Here, he said, was Colonel Gorgas, the world's foremost authority in the field of sanitation, taking orders from ignorant people who in turn were taking orders from people who knew nothing whatsoever about the problems at hand. He scornfully reproached the Commissioners for trying to foist false theories upon Gorgas, and took them particularly to task for their penuriousness and insistence on needless red tape.

As an example of this, he described the case of the destitute baby at the Ancon Hospital, whose nurse applied to Major La Garde for a rubber nipple and a nursing bottle. The Major had neither, because his order of the previous September had not yet been filled. He therefore made out a requisition, took it to Colonel Gorgas for his indorsement, presented it to Mr. Tobey, chief of the bureau of materials and supplies, for his indorsement, then took it to a clerk to have it copied and indorsed. Finally a messenger was permitted to go to a drug store and buy a nursing bottle and nipple. These reached the infant two days after the necessity for their use had arisen.

"The articles ought not to have cost more than thirty cents," reported Dr. Reed, "but counting the money value of the time of the nurse, of Major La Garde, of his clerical help, of Colonel Gorgas, of Mr. Tobey, of Mr. Tobey's clerks and of the messenger, the cost to the Government of the United States was in the neighborhood of $6.75—all due to the penny-wise-and-pound-foolish policy of the Commission. . . ."

The result of this report was electric. The shock was nowhere more clearly felt than in the White House where President Theodore Roosevelt with a stroke of a pen sacked every member of the Commission.

A new Canal Commission was set up, headed by an aggressive railroad builder named Theodore Shonts. At last it looked as though William Gorgas would be able to go peacefully about his work. Incredible as it may seem, however, neither Shonts nor Charles Magoon, another commissioner, believed in the mosquito theory of yellow fever. If Gorgas was doing a good job, they reasoned, why was there yellow fever in Panama? They heartily agreed that the whole Sanitation Department had to be shaken up and that Gorgas must go. Shonts had a friend, a Dr. Hamilton Wright, who he thought should take over Gorgas's job. Accordingly he lost no time asking the Secretary of War to dismiss Gorgas, Carter and all the others who believed in the mosquito theory.

The Secretary of War referred the request to the President, who was greatly disturbed that this matter had not been straightened out when he discharged the old Commission. What he personally knew about Gorgas and his work was all good. Not being an authority in medical matters, however, he wrote for advice to Walter Reed's teacher and friend, Dr. William Welch, Dean of the Johns Hopkins Medical School, adding: "I shall hold you responsible for every word you put in the letter." Welch replied that Dr. Wright, who had been recommended as Gorgas's successor, was competent enough for the job. But he also declared: "Your statement that you will hold me responsible for every word in this letter obliges me to add that in my opinion neither Dr. Wright nor anyone else is as well qualified to conduct this work as the present incumbent, Dr. Gorgas."

"Would to God," replied the President, "there were more men in America who had the moral courage to write honest letters of recommendation such as yours. . . ."

Because he wished to be absolutely sure of making the right decision, the President also sought advice from his friend and hunting companion, Dr. Alexander Lambert of New York City. Lambert had frequently stressed to the President the importance of controlling disease on the Isthmus. An admirer of Gorgas and his work, Lambert had only recently suggested that the President make Gorgas one of the commissioners.

Dr. Lambert went to Oyster Bay, the President's home, where he spent an entire evening in conference with him.

"I have sent for you," said the President, "for a talk about your friend, Dr. Gorgas. As you know, I'm not satisfied."

"Why not?" Lambert asked.

"They tell me Gorgas spends all his time oiling pools and trying to kill mosquitoes. Commissioner

Shonts claims that he is not cleaning up Panama or Colon, that they smell as bad as ever, and he recommends Colonel Gorgas's removal. The Secretary of War has gone over the matter and acquiesces in the recommendation."

"What Shonts says is true," replied Dr. Lambert, "but removing smells and improving ordinary sanitation do not destroy mosquitoes. Nor will that alone wipe out the malaria and the yellow fever which the mosquitoes produce. We must exterminate these insects and eradicate the two diseases. We cannot build the Canal unless we do this. The decision is in your hands. It is for you to choose between the old and the new methods and the two ideas represented. You can back the old idea and clean out the smells and see your workmen die of malaria and yellow fever. Or you can first clean up the puddles and kill the mosquitoes and, after this is done, clean up the place by ordinary sanitary methods. If you do the latter, you will have a healthy personnel with which to build your Canal. The French failed because of the terrible death rate from yellow fever and malaria. My uncle, who was working with them, told me that of 500 young engineers who came from France and worked in the swamps, not one lived to draw his first month's pay. Without exception they were swept off by disease. Napoleon sold Louisiana to us because his army had been annihilated at Santo Domingo by yellow fever. You must choose between Shonts and Gorgas; you must choose between the old method and the new; you must choose between failure with mosquitoes and success without them.

"I feel sorry for you tonight, Mr. President," continued Dr. Lambert. "You are facing one of the greatest decisions in your career. My belief is that if you fall back upon the old methods of sanitation, you will fail just as the French failed. On the other hand, if you back up Gorgas and his ideas and let him make his campaign against mosquitoes, then you will get that Canal. There is only one way of controlling yellow fever and malaria and that is to eradicate the mosquitoes. But I can only give you my advice: you must decide for yourself."

As Lambert spoke, the President's eyes were fixed intently upon him, and when he had finished he said nothing for a moment. He was thinking deeply of the grave decision at hand. "It is queer," he said at length, "I never appreciated before how essential it was. But I do now. By George, I'll back up Gorgas and we will see it through!"

The President lost little time in proving that he was as good as his word. Summoned to the White House, Commissioner Shonts saw angry eyes behind the presidential glasses and heard first-hand the lashing of a famous tongue. "Now I want you to get back of Gorgas!" snapped the President, shaking his finger.

With the fate of Admiral Walker fresh in his mind, Shonts quickly changed his attitude toward Gorgas, who from then on found things entirely different on the Isthmus. In the final months of his campaign against the mosquitoes he got everything he wanted. As a result, he utterly banished yellow fever from the torrid Canal Zone.

In November, 1906, Roosevelt sailed to Panama to observe the progress of his beloved Canal, and to inspect the Sanitary Department over which there had been so much controversy. Arriving by train at Panama City in the middle of a wild tropical storm, he entered his carriage and disappeared in the confusion, much to the bewilderment of the United States authorities and police. They finally found him calmly going through Ancon Hospital with Colonel Gorgas.

During the next days the Doctor accompanied the tireless President on an inspection of virtually every station and camp in the Canal Zone. At one of them sanitary conditions were not what they should have been, owing to the negligence of one of the inspectors. Gorgas was sharply, and perhaps unduly, criticized by the President. "I have failed," Gorgas told his wife. "President Roosevelt has criticized my work. No doubt I shall be relieved at once."

He was still in this gloomy frame of mind when, in the midst of a throng of people, the President prepared to board the steamer for the United States. Taking a few steps on the dock, the President stopped suddenly and called out: "Where is Dr. Gorgas? I want to see Dr. Gorgas!" Quickly making their way through the crowd, the Colonel and his wife were warmly greeted by the President and Mrs. Roosevelt and asked to accompany them to the gangplank. As the Chief Executive went aboard, the Doctor whispered to his wife: "I don't think we'll pack our trunks just yet."

The furthest wish from the President's mind was that William Gorgas should pack his trunks. In his next address to Congress, Roosevelt recommended that the Doctor be made one of the Commissioners of the Canal. And it was so voted.

Thus did recognition come at last to Panama's devoted conqueror of yellow fever—a man who could never rest until he had made the Canal Zone one of the healthiest places in the world. During his final years on the Isthmus Colonel Gorgas worked unsparingly for the control of malaria. And when the Canal was nearly finished, it was appropriate that the man without whose work this colossal project must certainly have failed was the first to travel its waters from the Pacific to the Atlantic. Dr. Gorgas and Chief Inspector Le Prince made the trip in a canoe.

As the two men paddled their way toward Gaillard Cut, an Irishman shouted from the top of the steep embankment: "Wait a minute!

There's something I want to know! I never dreamed I'd live to see the first ship go through this cut! Tell me, where be ye goin'?"

"We're on our way to the Atlantic!" returned a voice from the tiny vessel far below.

"The Lord be praised!" shouted back the Irishman. "It's with me own eyes I've seen the first boat go acrost, and now I believe others can go!"

Carrying their canoe up the steep cliffs around unfinished locks, the adventurers continued their long journey to the East through deep pools and down the rapids of the Chagres River, soon to merge its waters with the man-made Gatun Lake. On and on the two men paddled with aching arms until at last they reached Colon and the Atlantic Ocean.

WILLIAM GORGAS
1854 -1920

13

THE KING PAYS HIS RESPECTS

"What would you do," asked Dr. Franklin H. Martin, a colleague of General Gorgas, "if tomorrow morning before arising you should receive a telephone message assuring you that the war was ended?"

"Do you know what I would do? I would ring

off," replied the General, "call New York City, and order a passage for South America. I would go to Guayaquil, Ecuador, where yellow fever is prevalent, exterminate the pestilence, and then return to Panama, the garden spot of the world, and end my days writing about yellow fever."

Thus, at the height of his duties as Surgeon-General of the United States Army during the First World War, spoke Major-General William Gorgas. When the Panama Canal was finished, he was 60 years old. His next post might well have been an easy chair, or a peaceful seat in the executive's office of some large university. He was offered two such presidencies, but chose instead a campaign against pneumonia in South Africa, and new assaults on yellow fever in Ecuador, Peru, Colombia, Venezuela, Brazil, Central America and Mexico.

Meanwhile President Wilson had appointed him Surgeon-General. When the First World War broke out, his was the task of increasing the number of doctors in the Army Medical Corps from 435 to 32,000 and recruiting 250,000 enlisted men and 22,000 nurses. Reorganizing the whole Army hospital system, he looked after the health of hundreds of thousands of sick and wounded men on two continents. That was a lot of work for any man, to say nothing of an old one.

And yet when the war was over and he retired from the service, he began to draw up new blueprints against yellow fever, for it was his desire to wipe it completely from the face of the earth. Fortunately he no longer had to work with his own bare hands as he had done in Cuba and Panama, and as Walter Reed had had to do in proving his theories to a doubtful world. For John D. Rockefeller had set up an institution to combat diseases in the four corners of the globe.

As chairman of the Yellow Fever Commission, a part of the International Health Board, it was up to General Gorgas to muster the medical forces of the Rockefeller Foundation, to plan the attack and to lead it. Since Yellow Jack was reported to be at large in the jungles of Africa, General Gorgas decided to go there himself to investigate. In May, 1920, he sailed for Europe en route to Africa. Upon his arrival in Belgium, the conqueror of yellow fever in Panama was awarded the Harbin gold medal in recognition of his services to mankind. As he visited with the King and Queen, he seemed in good health and spirits, yet very early the following morning he called his wife and calmly told her that he had just suffered a paralytic stroke.

He was moved to Queen Alexandra Military Hospital in London, where he rested comfortably in the care of England's finest doctors. Yet after a week or so he realized that he was not going to get better.

There was a flurry one morning in the sickroom that overlooked the Thames River—and throughout the whole hospital, actually—for word had been received that the King was coming. When informed that General Gorgas was critically ill, His Majesty had announced: "If General Gorgas is too ill to come to the palace to see me, I shall go to the hospital to see him." And so, with little ceremony, he came. Sitting at the bedside of William Gorgas, he talked of Cuba and Panama and the conquest of yellow fever. He thanked Gorgas for his help to the British Empire as Surgeon-General of the United States during the war.

Vividly recalling the scene, Marie Gorgas, the doctor's wife, wrote: "Then, taking from his Equerry the insignia of the Knight Commander of the Most Distinguished Order of St. Michael and St. George, the King presented it to Dr. Gorgas, saying: 'General Gorgas: it gives me very great pleasure to present you with the insignia of this Order; and believe me, I very sincerely appreciate the great work which you have done for humanity. . . .' "

14

VICTORY

The invader had been pushed back but not beaten, and two of medicine's giant figures, Reed and Gorgas, were gone. Who would continue the conquest? If the age of the specialist and of teamwork had not arrived the riddle of yellow fever might never have been completely solved. What strides could a few individuals, working alone, ever have made against a baffling disease which was now resisting even the imposing forces of the Rockefeller Foundation? After the First World War the International Health Board and the countries with which it coöperated spent millions of dollars in the yellow fever campaign. Several of its most eminent doctors fell victim to the disease in the slow, discouraging and seemingly endless search for a successful vaccine.

The first of the Foundation's efforts centered around the renowned bacteriologist, Hideyo Noguchi, whom General Gorgas sent to South America to investigate an epidemic in Ecuador. Six weeks after his arrival, Noguchi announced that he had isolated the mysterious marauder that coursed in the blood of the yellow fever victim. Such news, coming from Noguchi, was received with great excitement in America. From humble beginnings on a poverty-stricken Japanese farm Noguchi, in the few years since he had become a naturalized American, had made some really spectacular discoveries. He had helped to develop the first protective serum against the bite of the rattlesnake. He had added much to the knowledge of such diverse diseases as syphilis, smallpox, and infantile paralysis. If he now claimed he had found the spirochete causing yellow fever it must be so.

It was not, unfortunately. Noguchi was on the trail of a similar disease called leptospirosis, commonly known as Weil's Disease, whose symptoms are much like those of yellow fever. He later developed a vaccine which appeared to be successful but the facts still were that the disease he was treating was not yellow fever.

While many of Noguchi's colleagues were suspicious that he had been on the wrong trail, none of them had been able to prove it. And so, a quarter of a century after Walter Reed had proved that the mosquito is the carrier of yellow fever, medical science still had not isolated the virus that caused it, still had no protective vaccine, and still did not know why the disease broke out in the jungles. Whenever local epidemics were reported in Ecuador, Peru, Brazil, Honduras, El Salvador, Nicaragua and Mexico, Gorgas's tried-and-true mosquito brigades went to work. They were still science's only telling weapon.

Before General Gorgas died in 1919 he had been planning to go to Africa to find out if the disease reported there was the same Yellow Jack which he had combatted in Cuba, Panama and South America. A second Rockefeller Commission, arriving in Africa in 1925, finally found the key that unlocked the mystery. But before this, a whole year had been spent on experiment after experiment. At last the head of the Commission, Colonel Henry Beeuwkes, imported some Rhesus monkeys from India. On June 30, 1927, staff doctors A. F. Mahaffy and J. H. Bauer inoculated a monkey with the blood of a 28-year-old African named Asibi who was ill with yellow fever. The monkey contracted the disease four days later and died on the fifth. This was a tremendously important as well as a frightening discovery. It meant that mosquitoes could apparently carry yellow fever from monkey to monkey, and from monkey to man. The disease was not, therefore, mainly a city dweller. It was obviously capable of springing forth and ambushing a lone Negro in the jungle, or a whole village of natives and whites.

Since man could never wipe out all the fever-carrying monkeys and mosquitoes in the jungle, his only hope was to intensify the search for the mysterious germ and find a vaccine which could immunize whole populations in tropical countries. This is, of course, a defensive, not an offensive measure. It can be compared with the procedure adopted by dwellers of the Mississippi Valley, who cannot hope to rid the river of floods. Instead they must be prepared at all times to sand-bag the dikes.

One very favorable outcome of the new discovery was that henceforth monkeys—and not men—could be used in experiments. A research scientist's task is always vastly simplified if some animal is also susceptible to the disease in question. By allowing infected mosquitoes to bite monkeys, thus carrying Yellow Jack from animal to animal, Adrian Stokes, a British doctor working in Africa with the International Health Board (together with Doctors Bauer and Hudson) showed how the disease could be kept alive in a remote area where there were no people. The doctors were also able to prove that the agent responsible for yellow fever was a filterable virus, one capable of passing through a fine filter such as porcelain. (This is true also of polio, influenza and many other diseases.) So Walter Reed had been right back in 1901 when he surmised that "a micro-organism so minute in size that it might be designated as ultramicroscopic" was the cause of yellow fever.

The year 1927, a towering landmark in the conquest of the ancient scourge, did not pass without tragedy. Adrian Stokes died of yellow fever.

Apparently he was not bitten by a mosquito. Associates believe that he spilled a virus suspension (dispersion of the virus in a liquid) which may have penetrated his skin. In a last measure of defiance, as if it were making three wise men pay for the secrets it had given up to them, Yellow Jack also claimed the lives of colleagues William Young and Hideyo Noguchi. There was as much triumph as tragedy in the passing of these men. Like Dr. Lazear many years before, they lost their lives in the conquest of a vicious disease. Were it not for their sacrifices thousands who are living today would be dead.

Unsolved problems still remained but Yellow Jack was now definitely in flight. Since the scientists knew the identity of their enemy—a virus (the same virus in Africa and South America)—they could now greatly intensify their efforts to find a vaccine. In 1930 Dr. Max Theiler of the Harvard Medical School discovered that white mice are susceptible to yellow fever. This was a far better animal to experiment with than the difficult Rhesus monkey. Building upon the great blocks of knowledge laid down by many scientists of many countries, the doctors at last emerged triumphantly with a vaccine called 17-D. It could be produced in tremendous quantities and provide millions of people with immunity against Yellow Jack.

Without having to understand the complicated techniques involved, we can appreciate why it took ten more years, until 1936, to produce 17-D. In a 710-page book on yellow fever edited by Dr. George K. Strode of the Rockefeller Foundation the triumph of a successful vaccine is described. We learn that yellow fever virus from the blood serum of Asibi, the African who became infected with the disease, was grown in a succession of different culture media. This included such seemingly odd materials as ground-up mouse embryo, minced chicken embryo, and blood serum obtained from a monkey. Hundreds of separate steps were taken to purify the virus so that it would be both stable and potent. The resulting strain was designated as 17-D.

During the long, rewarding years of search for a successful vaccine, doctors had been groping for an explanation as to why yellow fever existed in areas where the domestic mosquito—*Aedes aegypti* —was not present. In 1928 Dr. Bauer and several other scientists working in Africa and South America found that several kinds of mosquitoes other than *A. aegypti* could transmit yellow fever. This complicated matters, for world-wide control of several kinds of mosquitoes was obviously impossible. Nevertheless the discovery brought a whole series of new investigations which led to new discoveries.

Yellow fever broke out in a valley in Brazil where there was not a single *A. aegypti*. Investigators from the Brazilian National Health Service and the International Health Board first found that most of the victims were men. This was strange because in all other epidemics the disease attacked both sexes, young and old, indiscriminately. Further study revealed an interesting fact: all the stricken men worked in the forests. An analysis of the mosquito population there produced a likely suspect—*Haemagogus spegazzinii*—which, along with the monkeys, lived in the canopy of the forest.

Pursuing this lead, the investigators found that the native forest-workers caught Yellow Jack in a logical but most unlikely way. The forest mosquito was not only rare but virtually non-existent on the ground where the natives worked. However, when they felled a tree the leafy canopy came crashing down, bringing scores of *Haemagogus spegazzinii* with it. Fever-carrying mosquitoes, having consorted with the monkey population, now attacked the woodsmen and a human epidemic was under way.

After years of effort scientists succeeded in catching some infected mosquitoes and having them bite and infect some captured monkeys with what had come to be called Jungle Yellow Fever. All that was now necessary to prove that *Haemagogus spegazzinii* was a carrier was to find the deadly virus present among both the mosquito and monkey populations at the same time. In 1940 this last link of proof was produced.

In Africa Jungle Yellow Fever followed the same pattern, although with different variations. There, the guilty mosquito was found to be *Aedes Africanus.* Infected monkeys occasionally would steal from the edge of the deep forests and invade the plantations of the natives. Here they were bitten by a local mosquito, *Aedes sympsoni,* which in turn passed Yellow Jack along to the inhabitants.

The organized fight against Yellow Jack has been going on since 1900 and is not over yet. The vaccine 17-D is a priceless ally of humanity, yet

it is virtually impossible to vaccinate every inhab-
itant of Africa and South America and the other
tropical countries where the disease still exists.
And, as has been said, it is even more difficult to
stamp it out among the monkey population, for
this could only be done by completely annihilating
every mosquito in the world.

Still, much headway has been made at least
against the very dangerous domestic mosquito.
There are certain vigilant countries in South
America where not a single *A. aegypti* exists. As
a result, an outbreak of Yellow Jack is extremely
unlikely in those countries, especially as the rarer
forest mosquitoes do not inhabit the villages. But
the forest mosquito is responsible for the fact that
the ancient disease has been creeping up Central
America in the monkey population. An emigrant
with yellow fever, arriving in Louisiana or Texas
from South America, could of course pass the
infection along to the domestic mosquitoes which

abound in our southern states. Even so, an epidemic of any size would be most unlikely, for we now know the habits of Yellow Jack.

And we have the crusading doctors of the Rockefeller Foundation, along with many scientists of Latin America, Europe and Africa to thank for much of what we know. Between 1918 and 1949 the Foundation's International Health Board spent nearly 14 millions of dollars in 14 countries and engaged the services of 76 staff doctors against yellow fever alone. Among the many medical pioneers engaged in this seemingly endless fight, the names of Carlos Finlay, Walter Reed and William Gorgas still stand out boldly.

Some years before Sir William's death, an Army general was walking down Connecticut Avenue in Washington with his granddaughter when he chanced to meet William Gorgas. "This is General Gorgas," he said to his granddaughter, "one of our great men."

"No," said Gorgas, "merely one who is trying

to follow in the footsteps of a great man—Walter Reed." The College of Electors of the Hall of Fame agreed, for in 1945 they voted that Reed's name join those of less than one hundred of the most illustrious Americans.

On what was once the farm of Dr. Ignacio Rojas near Los Quemados, Cuba, a weathered shack still stands. It is Building Number 1, where in the anxious days of early winter in the year 1900 Walter Reed proved that infected clothing and bedding did not spread yellow fever.

A grander memorial, suggesting quite as much in terms of the saving of human life, was built in 1909 by the United States Congress on a tract of land near the northern border of the District of Columbia. It is today a vast city of medicine where six thousand persons are at work in war and peace caring for the health of the United States Army.

The shining corridors of its 292 buildings symbolize the advances man has made during a single generation in his dramatic march against disease. It is fitting that it is called the Walter Reed Army Medical Center, "honoring the memory of the medical officer whose researches in yellow fever are by far the most important contributions to science which have ever come from an Army surgeon. . . ."

BIBLIOGRAPHY

AGRAMONTE, ARISTIDES, Yellow fever prophylaxis. *Journal of Tropical Medicine*, 27: 285-287, 1924.

ARMSTRONG, GEORGE E., The work of Dr. Walter Reed. (Talk delivered at the Hall of Fame, New York University on May 20, 1948.) Washington: Department of the Army, Surgeon-General's Office, 1948.

BAUER, J. H., Transmission of yellow fever by mosquitoes other than *Aedes aegypti*. *American Journal of Tropical Medicine*, 8: 261-282, 1928.

——— AND MAHAFFY, A. F., Susceptibility of African monkeys to yellow fever. *American Journal of Hygiene*, 12: 155-174, 1930.

CARROLL, J., Yellow Fever. Ch. 27, pp. 736-759 in *A System of Medicine* edited by Osler, W. and McCrae, T. London: Oxford University Press, 1907.

CHAMBERLAIN, WESTON P., *Twenty-five Years of American Medical Activity on the Isthmus of Panama, 1904-1929.* The Panama Canal Press, 1929.

CARTER, HENRY ROSE, Yellow fever—its nature, diagnosis, treatment and prophylaxis, and quarantine regulations pertaining thereto. Washington: Treasury Department, U.S. Marine Hospital Service (pp. 339-357), 1899.

——, A note on the interval between infecting and secondary cases of yellow fever at Orwood and Taylor, Miss., 1898. *New Orleans Medical and Surgical Journal*, 52: 617-636, 1900.

——, Yellow fever mortality in Havana, 1884-1900, statistics and deductions. Public Health Reports, U.S. Marine Hospital Service, 15: 1840-1853, 1900.

——, The methods of the conveyance of yellow fever infection. In Bulletin No. 10, Yellow Fever Institute. Washington: Government Printing Office, 1902.

———, *Yellow Fever, an Epidemiological and Historical Study of its Place and Origin.* Baltimore: Williams & Wilkins, 1931.

FINLAY, CARLOS JUAN, *Trabajos Selectos.* (A compilation from various journals of Finlay's early [1881-1907] writings on yellow fever.) Havana: 1912.

[1881-1907] writings on yellow fever.)

FINLAY, CARLOS EDUARDO JOSÉ, *Carlos Finlay and Yellow Fever.* New York: Oxford University Press, 1940.

GIBSON, JOHN M., *Physician to the World: The life of General William C. Gorgas.* Durham, N.C.: Duke University Press, 1950.

GORGAS, MARIE D., *William Crawford Gorgas, His Life and Work.* New York: Doubleday Page & Co., 1924.

GORGAS, W. C., A few general directions with regard to destroying mosquitoes, particularly the yellow fever kind. Washington: Government Printing Office, 1904.

———, *Sanitation in Panama.* New York: D. Appleton & Co., 1915.

HENCH, PHILIP SHOWALTER, *Conquerors of yellow fever.* *Hygeia,* Vol. 19, No. 10, 1941.

——, Walter Reed and the conquest of yellow fever. Reprinted from *Pharos of Alpha Omega Alpha,* May, 1948.

——, Walter Reed and the conquest of yellow fever. Proceedings of the 4th International Congress on Tropical Medicine and Malaria, May, 1948.

——, Kissinger, John R., Interview with Dr. Phillip S. Hench.

——, Moran, John J., Interview with Dr. Phillip S. Hench.

——, Reed, Walter, Autographed letters to his wife in possession of Dr. Hench.

KEAN, JEFFERSON RANDOLPH, The scientific work and discoveries of the late Maj. Walter Reed, surgeon in the Army of the United States. Washington: Government Printing Office, 1903.

KELLY, HOWARD A., *Walter Reed and Yellow Fever.* New York: McClure, Phillips & Co., 1906.

REED, WALTER; CARROLL, JAMES; AGRAMONTE, ARISTIDES AND LAZEAR, JESSE W., The etiology of yellow fever; a preliminary note. Proceedings of the American Public Health Association, 1900.

——, Yellow fever. Senate document 822, U.S. 61st Congress, 3rd session. (Contains seven articles by the Yellow Fever Board.) Washington: U.S. Government Printing Office, 1911.

RUSH, BENJAMIN, An inquiry into the various sources of the usual forms of summer and autumnal disease in the United States, and the means of preventing them; to which are added facts intended to prove the yellow fever not to be contagious. Philadelphia: J. Conrad & Co., 1805.

SAWYER, W. A., History of the activities of the Rockefeller Foundation in investigation and control of yellow fever. *American Journal of Tropical Medicine*, 17: 35-50, 1937.

SOPER, F. L., Present day methods for study and control of yellow fever. *American Journal of Tropical Medicine*, 17: 655-676, 1937.

STERNBERG, GEORGE MILLER, The transmission of yellow fever by mosquitoes. *Popular Science Monthly*, July, 1901.

STRODE, GEORGE K., editor, *Yellow Fever*. New York: McGraw Hill Book Co., 1951.

TRUBY, ALBERT E., *Memoir of Walter Reed*. New York: P. B. Hoeber, Inc., 1943.

WEBSTER, NOAH, (Letter) to the physicians of Philadelphia, New York, Baltimore, Norfolk, and New Haven, Oct. 31, 1795 (in Webster, N., Letters; edited by H. R. Warfel. New York: Library Publishers, 1954).

WOOD, LAURA N., *Walter Reed, Doctor in Uniform*. New York: Julian Messner, Inc., 1943.

INDEX

177

Index

Index

LANDMARK BOOKS

WORLD LANDMARK BOOKS